P9-AFI-647

ESSAYS ON THE NATURE OF ART

ESSAYS ON THE NATURE OF ART

by
Eliot Deutsch

State University of New York Press

Published by
State University of New York Press, Albany

Printed in the United State of America

For information, address the State University of New York Press, State University Plaza, Albany, NY 12246

Library of Congress Cataloging-in-Publication Data

Deutsch, Eliot.
Essays on the nature of art / Eliot Deutsch.
p. cm.
Includes bibliographical references and index.
ISBN 0-7914-3111-8 (alk. paper). -- ISBN 0-7914-3112-6 (pbk. : alk. paper)
1. Art--Philosophy. 2. Aesthetics. I. Title.
BH39.D456 1996
700'.1--dc20 95-26407
CIP

10 9 8 7 6 5 4 3 2 1

to

Leroy S. Rouner
Roger T. Ames
Henry Rosemont, Jr.

Inspiring Friends

who embody so fully the philosophical virtues of devoted service, spiritual insight, and intellectual honesty

CONTENTS

Preface

I am concerned in this work to develop a very broad, if not comprehensive, conception of what art is, both as a universal activity and as a localized practice that is culturally informed and historically grounded. This work, then, will present at once an essentialist account of the nature of an artwork and a contextualized characterization of aesthetic experience and the role of art in society. I will argue that art enjoys a special kind of autonomy while at the same time having profound social and political responsibilities.

The work is divided into three parts. Part I articulates a general definition of art in answer to the basic question "What is art?" I show that art can be seen to have as its intentionality the striving to be aesthetically forceful, meaningful, and beautiful, with the artwork, the manner of its coming into being, and the experience of it constituting an integral whole. The short nonconnected essays in Part II address several aspects of some of the particular arts (e.g., poetry, dance, music) in such a way as, ideally, to deepen an understanding of the more abstract concepts and notions put forward in the first part. These essays do not in any way attempt to constitute a systematic aesthetics of the arts as such. Part III explores a number of interconnected themes having to do with the controversial issues of art interpretation, truth in art, and the complex relations between art and morality and art and religion.

I am grateful to many colleagues and friends for their advice and encouragement in the preparation of this work. I am especially grateful to my very good friends to whom this work is dedicated, for their unstinting support over many years, and to my wife, Marcia Morse—artist, teacher, and art critic—who always, with exquisite tact, extends challenges that call for subtle revisions in one's thinking.

I also wish to thank the University of Hawaii Press and the University of Notre Dame Press for permission to incorporate in several sections early versions of some materials previously published by them.

Part I

1

On the Question "What Is Art?"

Philosophically, the question "What is art?" is often addressed in an ahistorical manner, as if artworks themselves were not deeply embedded in their cultural matrices and could resist being an integral part of those matrices. The political/social structures and values of a society, however, and its ontological commitments, as it were, do quite obviously inform artistic practices throughout history and contribute significantly to answers given to the question "What is art?" One need only look to the social standing of the artist and the "for whom" and under what conditions the artwork was intended to be viewed and appreciated in different times and places to see how these contributed to any given society's self-understanding of what a work of art is.

In the West alone there has been a remarkable transition from the time when the artist was a rather lowly craftsman (in Greece, especially if the artist were a practitioner of one of the "mechanical" arts, those that required an immense expenditure of physical effort), to his being a member of a respected, if not highly rewarded, guild; to his or her becoming a member of the artworld, subservient, first to aristocratic and royal taste and then to various market considerations and other social/political constraints. In between, of course, the artist was a "genius" asserting his or her own radical, and often antibourgeois, independence.

We clearly get fundamentally different attitudes toward what a work of art should be when there is an educated, leisure class for whom the work is essentially an object for aesthetic contemplation, the viewer becoming, or aspiring to be, as in traditional Confucian China, a "connoisseur," and when, say in the medieval Christian West, with a hieratic, theologically oriented society, the viewer is regarded to be cognitively deficient, the artwork then becoming a means to overcome that deficiency.

When, as in more recent times, artworks became personal property they acquired a new kind of autonomy. Instead of being public works or otherwise "owned" by church or ruler, they became separate, distinct entities that could be bought, sold, exchanged, stolen, and, in some circumstances, lawfully destroyed.

Kim Levin, an art critic, although overstating somewhat her point, notes that "Because it [Modernist art] was competitive and individualistic, it saw everything in terms of risk. Like capitalism, it was materialistic. From its collage scraps and fur-lined teacups to its laden brushstrokes, I-beams, and Campbell's soup cans, Modernist art insisted increasingly on being an object in a world of objects. What started as radical physicality turned into commodity; the desire for newness led to a voracious appetite for novelty."[1] And the individual arts did, under varying social circumstances, acquire their fundamental independence from extra-aesthetic demands at different times and places. Lydia Goehr has pointed out that

> For most of its history, music was conceived as a practice entirely subject to the constraints of extra-musical occasion and function determined mostly by the church, court and scientific community. The changes that took place at the end of the eighteenth century gave rise to a new view of music as an independent practice whose concerns were predominately musical. This independent practice became a practice geared toward producing *enduring products* insofar as it was determined by the more general concepts of fine art and the autonomous work of art. Only with the rise of this new view of music did musicians, critics, and the like begin to think predominately of music in terms of works. Bach did not think centrally in these terms; Beethoven did. Haydn makes the transition.[2]

With painting, sculpture, and architecture, on the other hand, "autonomy" was apparently achieved to a considerable degree at an earlier Renaissance and post-Renaissance time. Still, with the rise of the private art collector and then of museums, an artwork tended to become part of a gathering and to lose thereby something of its unique, individual power and status. An artwork, a modern artist might well proclaim, wants to be a world—not a part of a collection of things.

Consider also the differences historically as to who was allowed, and under what circumstances, admittance to the performing arts. In ancient Greece, where theater was a communal, ritualistic affair as much as it was a "tragedy" or "comedy," admittance was by citizenship—and not everyone was a citizen. In the eighteenth century musical occasions were for small intimate gatherings, with admittance by invitation. Today, with public concerts and the like, admittance is for anyone with payment. Surely these respective social situations had some direct connection not only with the kind of art produced but to the very conception in those societies regarding what a work of art is. Did it intend to promote certain communal values, or be an occasion for, and thereby subservient to, a display of class interest and power, or be a kind of entertainment, an escape from otherwise humdrum being?

In short, we can, I think, agree with Frank Burch Brown who states that "The aesthetic object is constituted not just by *what* is seen but by *how* it is seen—that is, by what it is seen *as*—which depends partly on its whole milieu, including the contexts of perception and various things that we know or think we know."[3]

And among the things "we know or think we know" are various structures of being within which, among other factors, we frame our views of what art is. Another way of putting this would be to say that any theory of art or systematic reflection on the subject is always developed against the background of an ontology, stated or not, and its attendant epistemological and axiological claims; for any discussion of what art is can be addressed only through various presuppositions concerning what there is in general and the manner of being of that "what" and how it is known.

Referring to Augustine and Bernard of Clairvaux, for example, Brown argues that their "negative bias against what today we term the aesthetic and the artistic" is intelligible only against the background of the "dubious and originally non-Christian idea from the late Classical and Hellenistic world that there is an ontological hierarchy—a great chain or ladder of being—ascent of which requires that the devout spirit and truth-seeking mind progressively leave behind things of body and sense. It is this particular hierarchy and this view of human nature," he goes on to say, "that prevents any acknowledgement that something so sensory as art could provide a true standard or norm for religious awareness and insight."[4]

In other words, and in short, there can be no aesthetics without ontology (and epistemology); for any analysis of what an artwork is and the experience appropriate to it will necessarily presuppose attitudes toward, if not deep claims about, the way "ordinary things" are and how they are known to be connected and interrelated with one another, and ideas about what human nature itself is.

Further, it is obvious that, as Roland Barthes writes, "the appearance of new technical means . . . modifies not only art's forms but its very concept."[5] The very term *art*, we know, derives from the Greek *technē* (and its Latin equivalent *ars*) and, for the Greeks, referred to a rich variety of human makings, to anything, in fact, that involved a learned skill, as in medicine, the crafts, or law. "Classifications of the arts" have undergone many changes in Western experience alone,[6] and it is not surprising, therefore, that a number of contemporary thinkers are convinced that art is simply an "open concept," or as Theodor Adorno puts it, "that, for the plurality of what are called 'the arts,' there does not even seem to exist a universal concept of art able to accommodate them all."[7]

Nevertheless, the question "What is art?" can be, and indeed has been, addressed at several different levels and kinds of generality. It may be dealt with as a problem in systematic philosophy and accordingly answered in overarching metaphysical terms (Hegelian-like: "Art is a spiritual activity of man which is delivered from a sensuous medium and contains an end bound up with it"); or it may be dealt with somewhat more empirically, art being characterized by those features that supposedly set artworks apart from other objects or that appropriately elicit a special response or "aesthetic experience."

It has often been recognized, however, the question itself presents linguistic and logical difficulties that seem to rule out any fruitful answer to it. First of all, it might be that what we accept as works of art is so extraordinarily rich and diverse, including as it does exquisite Chinese vases and mammoth Gothic cathedrals, simple songs and elaborate symphonies, abstract paintings, statues of gods and portraits of kings, that what is true about, or holds for, all objects in the class is very little indeed and not very interesting. Further, the question seems always to have been asked (and answered) relative to the art of a particular cultural time and place. The very import of the question "What is art?", in other words, is culture bound—and perhaps inescapably so. Also, the question appears to invite not so much a description of what art is as a prescription of what art ought to be. Underlying the answer to the question is usually a call or a program for what the answerer believes art ought to be (e.g., as in Tolstoy's famous essay entitled "What Is Art?"[8]).

Following Wittgenstein, some aestheticans (notably Morris Weitz) have also argued that it is impossible to formulate a conception of art through articulating necessary and sufficient properties of artworks; it is logically impossible, they say, to define art by any set of essential features that distinguish artworks from everything else. "The problem of the nature of art is like that of the nature of games, at least in these respects: If we actually look and see what it is that we call 'art', we will also find no common properties—only strands of similarities. Knowing what art is is not apprehending some manifest or latent essence but being able to recognize, describe and explain those things we call 'art' in virtue of these similarities."[9] 'Art,' the argument goes, is an "open concept"; that is, "its conditions of application are emendable and corrigible."

Maurice Mandelbaum, in his well-known article "Family Resemblances and Generalization Concerning the Arts,"[10] has nicely criticized this view by pointing out that to claim "family resemblance" only (as defined by Wittgenstein) for works of art overlooks the fact that there is an attribute common to all who bear a family resemblance, although it is not necessarily one among those characteristics that are directly exhibited—namely, common ancestry. Artworks may have "relational attributes" of this sort—although it might indeed be extraordinarily difficult to articulate them. Also that the artworld is not closed to new and different forms does not, as Weitz seemed to think, mean that 'art' is necessarily an "open concept." Future instances to which the concept of art may apply can, of course, possess genuinely novel properties, but the instances may nevertheless still come under a properly formed definition or general concept of art.

In his later thinking on these problems, Morris Weitz acknowledges that he

> identified the openness of the concept of art with its open texture [and] . . . assimilated all the subconcepts of art, such as tragedy, to Waismann's notion of open texture. Neither "art" nor any of its subterms, "tragedy," "drama," "music," "painting," etc. could be defined, since their criteria had to allow for the possibility of new ones that render definitive sets of them violations of the concepts they convey.
>
> The wholesale reading of open concepts in aesthetics as open texture concepts was a mistake.[11]

Weitz nevertheless continued to maintain that we can happily dispense with any "essentialist" account of what art is in favor of having "reasons that relate to disjunctive sets of nonnecessary, nonsufficient criteria and to their corresponding properties in the works of art that have them."[12]

The most radical formulation of an antiessentialist approach, however, is perhaps that put forward by George Dickie and others who, following Arthur Danto in his elaboration of the notion of an "artworld"[13]—only later to be repudiated by Danto in favor of the rather odd view that art, having reached full self-consciousness Hegelian-like in the minds of a number of contemporary urban artists, no longer has a "history"[14]—argue that a work of art is not to be defined by any qualities (family resemblancelike or otherwise) it may possess but simply according to what (certain) persons are willing to call a work of art within a certain social or institutional context. If a museum exhibits a pile of dirt thrown randomly on the floor with someone's (presumably the thrower's) signature attached to it, then it simply is a work of art in virtue of that investure. The concept 'work of art' thus applies to anything artifactual that is legitimized (baptized) in the artworld as a bearer of the concept. Dickie sums-up his 1974 version of the theory in these terms: "A work of art in the classificatory sense is (1) an artifact (2) a set of the aspects of which has had conferred upon it the status of a candidate for appreciation by some person or persons acting on behalf of a certain social institution (the artworld)."[15] He then offers a revised claim to the effect that "works of art are art as the result of the position or place they occupy within an established practice, namely, the artworld" and defines a *work of art* as "an artifact of a kind created to be presented to an artworld public."[16]

In delivering roundhouse blows against this theory, Richard Wollheim notes facetiously that "Painters make paintings, but [according to the theory] it takes a representative of the artworld to make a work of art."[17] Wollheim then poses what has to be taken as a crucial question and finds the "institutional theory" unable to address it satisfactorily.

> A question to put to the theory, which nicely divides its supporters into the faint-hearted and the bold, is this: Do the representatives of the art-world have to have, or do they not have to have, reasons for what they do if what they do is to stick? Is their status enough for them to be able to confer status upon what they pick out, or must they additionally exercise judgment, or taste, or critical acumen, so that it is only if the paintings they pick out satisfy certain criteria or meet certain conditions that status is transferred?

Wollheim, and now Danto as well, argue (on quite different grounds) that an artwork must indeed have certain qualities or be part of an interpretative network of relations, the recognition of which requires very much an exercise of judgment and critical acumen.

The answer then to "What is art?" is not to found by either turning away from the question or appealing to the role of (certain members of) institutions, but by *looking deeper.*

2

Art Is Imitation

The earliest philosophical theory in the West about art is that art is a kind of imitation (*mimesis*). Plato (in *The Republic* Bk. X) interpreted *mimesis* as "copying": the artist was concerned, Plato argued, to represent sense objects by a replication of their sensuous properties. With respect to poetry, Plato also argued (in *The Republic* Bk. III) that the office of the poet was to portray the doings of the gods correctly; the poets generally failed to do so and therefore their work was to be rejected on moral grounds. Aristotle, on the other hand, who thought that imitation was instinctive in man, developed a somewhat more sophisticated use of *mimesis* and seemed to argue that art imitated primarily the typical or universal dimensions of actions, characters, or events, disclosing thereby their general significance and also, so it has been suggested, nature's own productive activity or principle. "What art imitates," writes W. D. Ross, "is 'characters and emotions and actions'—not the sensible world, but the world of man's mind. Of all the arts the least imitative, that which can least be charged with merely trying to duplicate something already existing, is music; but for Aristotle it is the *most* imitative."[1]

It was left for Plotinus, however, the more ardent follower of Plato, to reject explicitly Plato's restriction of artistic imitation to the copying of sense objects. Plotinus insisted that the soul can rise to the principle of Beauty and that Beauty, as well as other Ideas, can be reflected in the mind of man as eternal models for his creativity. The arts, Plotinus writes, "gives no bare reproduction of the thing seen but go back to the Reason-Principles from which Nature itself derives, and, furthermore, that much of their work is all their own; they are holders of beauty and add where nature is lacking."[2]

The neoclassicism of the seventeenth century, however, which once again called for art to imitate nature, neglected the Plotinian interpretation in favor of the notion that imitation meant a rule-bound following of the general structures of things. *Verisimilitude* came to mean an imitation of ideal types. As applied to the human scene: "for a painter or poet, not actual men and actions with their baffling mixture of good and bad, but types of characters and purified logized fables leading in a way analogous to the syllogism to a consent of the mind, and to virtuous deeds, composed the true model in nature."[3]

After having been largely set aside under the impact of romanticism, "imitation" in recent times has again been seen by some scholars and critics to be a central concern in art. Leo Steinberg, for instance, has argued that "art through the ages shows unmistakably that most of it is dedicated precisely to the imitation of nature, to likeness-catching, to the portrayal of objects and situations—in short, to representation." Steinberg inveighs against those who interpret representation as "an adventitious element in art—a concession made to populace or church" or those who insist that "modern art, by eschewing the outgoing reference, constitutes something radically new and different" in favor of holding that "modern art has not, after all, abandoned the imitation of nature, and that, in its most powerful expressions, representation is still an essential condition, not an expendable freight."[4]

Susanne K. Langer, on the other hand, has observed that

> It is natural enough, perhaps, for naive reflection to center first of all round the relationship between an image and its object; and equally natural to treat a picture, statue, or a graphic description as an imitation of reality. The surprising thing is that long after art theory has passed the naive stage, and every serious thinker realized that imitation was neither the aim nor the measure of artistic creation, the traffic of the image with its model kept a central place among philosophical problems of art. It has figured as the question of form and content, of interpretation, of idealization, of belief and make-believe, and of impression and expression. Yet the idea of copying nature is not even applicable to all the arts. What does a building copy? On what given object does one model a melody?[5]

"Painting is an activity," E. H. Gombrich notes, "and the artist will therefore tend to see what he paints rather than paint what he sees."[6] Gombrich goes on to observe that "there is no neutral naturalism. The artist, no less than the writer, needs a vocabulary before he can embark on a 'copy' of reality."[7]

It seems evident that for imitation theory distinctions between *copy*, *resemble* and *represent* need to be carefully drawn. Too often, as with Steinberg, the terms get conflated and confused.

To copy in art means to replicate an object or other image with the intent to show that object or image in a particular medium as it is in its given real or presumed sensuous being. The copyist, in a self-effacing way, strives for—and indeed sometimes comes close, as in trompe l'oeil works, to realizing—the ideal of a *noninterpretive* seeing (an "innocent eye") and the embodiment of it in the materials of his or her medium. The possibility or impossibility of ever achieving a "true" or "faithful" copy of something rests then, at least partially, on the question of whether or not seeing is always interpretative, involving conceptual schemes, linguistic structures, categorical forms and the like; in short, a "vocabulary."

There does seem to be considerable agreement today among philosophers, both of realist and antirealist bent, and psychologists, of various persuasions, that to notice, to perceive, to regard (let alone to attend aesthetically) always calls for, to begin with, a certain *selectivity* that reflects the interests and values of the perceiver as well as the (sometimes, to be sure, intrusive) presence of the object seen. All seeing is mediated by one's past experience, one's knowledge of that which is being seen, and one's "sorting" (to use Nelson Goodman's term) of things within various linguistic schemata, and so on. There are no neutral perceptions of "mere things" (contra Arthur Danto)[8] on which interpretations are superadded: Seeing and interpreting are integral, both psychologically and epistemically.

And for art, rather ironically—and Aristotle perhaps realized this—the closer we come, without ever being able to achieve it fully, to having an innocent eye, the less aesthetic interest its embodiment will have for us, because that embodiment, like an image shown in a perfect mirror, will tend to lack a reality of its own.

Renaissance painting, nevertheless, according to Vasari, in contrast to medieval art, aspired precisely to a "true representation of the external world." But what does this aspiration really mean? What, to begin with, is the object of this "true representation," this "imitation"? Steinberg speaks of an "accurate transcription of the sensible world," which "sensible world" he then equates with "nature"—and, by implication in this context, with "reality."[9] But sensing the futility in any possible attempt to present such an "accurate transcription," Steinberg shifts direction and moves toward some kind of symbolic representation as being the essence of imitation. He defines it (almost Gombrich-like) as "the skill of reproducing handy graphic symbols for natural appearances, of rendering familiar facts by set professional conventions."[10] And art does this presumably through some kind of a relation of resemblance.

Resemblance, it is often noted, is a *transitive* relation: If X resembles Y, then (analytically?) Y resembles X. "Imitation," on the other hand, is said to be *intransitive*: The "original" does not imitate the "copy." Often in everyday language, however—especially when two things are of different kinds—we do speak as if resemblance were intransitive as well. When a cloud patterns resembles ("looks like") a human face, we do not say that the human face also looks like the cloud. The primary object, as it were, the cloud, dominates the relationship.

In any event, whereas resemblance may be—but often is not—*intentional*, imitation (however understood) always is. It makes no sense to us to say that one thing imitates another by sheer coincidence.

And the same holds for "representation." "To represent" something or other implies (unless one believes in some kind of occult doctrine of "natural affinities") an intentional symbolic depiction, one that frequently, but not necessarily, involves resemblance.

Let us take a child (say, a friend's son) and a portrait of him made by a well-known artist. We "read" both of these; that is to say, we "interpret" both the child and the portrait, but we do so in rather different ways. What does this tell us about the nature of "representation"?

The child is certainly no "mere thing"—for we always respond to him, as indeed to any human being, across a wide range of interests and values. At one end, say, with the face of a stranger who offers nothing of special interest to one, the reading might indeed be perfunctory, amounting to not much more than the registering of the fact that this object is a human being whom one does not know or have any further cares about (that "registering" nevertheless involving a rich cognitive bringing forth of various categories and the like). At the other end, say with that of our friend's son in whom one takes a great deal of spontaneous interest, the reading will be multivalent and complex.

First of all, in the very act of my recognizing that the child before me is my friend's son, there is a kind of conformity between my concept of the child and his appearance to me. This is just bare-bones recognition, but in this case a certain deeper interest simultaneously occurs in the act of recognition. I wonder if he is happy or troubled, in good health, and so on, noticing the changes in his appearance since I last saw him. I might try to read ahead, as it were, wondering what he will look like ten years from now. I also, in my reading, perform a complex series of immediate evaluations regarding my friend's son; evaluations directed to everything from his style of dress to his manners.

Let us look now at the portrait of the child by the well-known artist. With the portrait, as with the person, there is an initial recognition, not that the child before me is my friend's son but that the face presented is of him; that is to say, the recognition that the face shown *represents* my friend's son. The mere recognition, however, is not an occasion for any special existential interest; for I know immediately that the portrait is but a portrait, an "illusion" and not the real thing.

This mere recognition, however, does involve the relationship of resemblance. Something must be shown in the painting that enables me, indeed invites if not compels me, to see the painting as a portrait of my friend's son. The portrait must show some qualities or properties associated with him, it must resemble him in some essential way, before I can see it as being of him.[11]

Our reading of the portrait is then carried out in a vocabulary quite different from that of our reading of the person. We would ask: Is the representation *well-executed*? Is it *insightful*? Does it *show* something about the child that we never fully realized before? Is it in a *style* that is in keeping with the artist's other work? How does it *compare* with other portraits, if they exist, of the child? A critic might point out that the lines are *sharply and clearly etched*, that the rendering is *somber and yet graceful*, the depiction as a whole being at once *elegant and forceful*.

The temporality of the portrait, although involving the past and future, is of a concentrated present and will, itself not being subject to change in the actual presentation of its subject matter, remain as a present showing throughout its existence. Future generations may indeed take a deep interest in the portrait as a work of art long after anyone cares about or even remembers who the child actually was. *Ars longa, vita brevis*.

With a portrait as a representation, then, we have resemblance but not copying. Now, of course, not all representation involves a direct resemblance between what is represented and an actual sensible object; many representations primarily present symbols that point to a range of meanings associated with them. Pictorially, a skull on a table in a painting of St. Jerome will indeed resemble what we believe a skull to be, but its main function is to conjure up associative meanings about mortality and the like. Representation can, then, traverse a wide spectrum from the concrete particular to the abstract universal (with things like skulls and other recognizable objects which may serve as symbols being somewhere in between)—and the more it moves to the latter pole the less assured we are of what is being represented, for there is less evident a basis of resemblance.

Also, it is obvious that in art something can resemble a nonexistent or fictitious object as well as a "real" one. We have pictures of unicorns and drawings of characters from novels: They resemble what we "know" of these nonconcretely actualized things.

In short, in spite of a given artist's intention to depict sensible reality accurately (or a theorist's argument that this is what the artist should be trying to do) it can readily be shown that the artist is always doing something different, namely, interpreting or representing, and doing so within culturally established conventions and canons (even when these conventions and canons are, at any given time, being challenged and revolutionized) and by means of specific materials and within culturally informed and personal stylistic constraints.

Representation, however, is no longer imitation in any usual sense of a copy/model relation and so we need to continue to look for a deeper sense of *imitation*, and we can, I believe, find it within the creative process of artwork making rather than exclusively in a relationship between what may be presented in the artwork and what may be external to it—its presumed "reference."

* * *

"In early Greece," Wladyslaw Tatarkiewicz observes, "*mimesis* signified imitation, but in the sense in which the term is applied to acting and not to copying."[12] Imitation in art, I want to argue, means properly an "acting out," a drawing from the very root of spiritual being so that the artwork can present or perform with power its own aesthetic content or meaning. To imitate in art, I believe, means properly to have the expressive content of the work grounded in reality. That work of art is most truly imitative which is a concentration of the power of spiritual being. To imitate in art thus means to be determined by reality at its most essential level. It means to have one's creative drive be in accord with—be derived from—a natural spiritual rhythm and power of being.

To be "grounded in," to be "rooted," means to be "tied to," which means rightly to be "influenced by": In the fullest sense of *influence*, it means to "partake of the essential character of" that which is the source of the influence. "Imitation" is thus a property, not a relation; which is to say that it is a quality become inherent in the artwork rather than something that obtains between the artwork and some object or process external to it.

Tatarkiewicz also noted that "Democritus understood it [*mimesis*] in the sense in which a pupil imitates a master."[13] Now although Democritus does not seem to have the human master/disciple relationship as his model ("we have been the pupils [of the animals] in matters of fundamental importance, of the spider in weaving and mending, of the swallow in home-building, of the sweet-voiced swan and nightingale in our imitation of their song"[14]), we can nevertheless learn something about the nature of imitation in terms of this relationship.

A pupil (disciple) does not simply copy or mimic the master but strives to appropriate to himself something of the special skill, power, and quality that the master possesses and embodies—and to do so in terms of the special conditions of his own being. Imitation by way of influence is a transmission without loss to the transmitter. It yields, when it is successful, a style appropriate to the one who receives the transmission.[15]

How, one might ask, does this work with the relation between artist and nature (or life or reality) that imitation theory has always concerned itself with in a primary way. Can it be rightly said that nature influences the artist? The answer, I believe, is yes.

Nature is that to which an artist is obedient, not in the sense of simple submission but in that of "coming into an accord with," allowing it, through the recognition of one's belonging with it, to empower one. Obedience here, then, is not a matter of dictation but of participation; it is, like all intersubjective experience, a reciprocal relationship. It becomes then an emulation, a value-recognizing activity; it becomes a celebration, a partaking of, an active receiving of spiritual vitality.

Imitation, in this sense, thus helps us to understood the assertion that a work of art is its own meaning; that art is autonomous. The assertion does not properly argue (as Clive Bell has done) that art need not draw anything from life and that "to appreciate a work of art we need bring with us nothing but a sense of form and color and knowledge of three-dimensional space."[16] Nor does it argue that a work of art should (or should not) have a recognizable subject matter, that it should (or should not) represent an identifiable something or other. It argues that the aesthetic content of the work, if it is to be meaningful, must, at its deepest level, bear the strength and confidence of its being influenced by one or more aspects or dimensions of reality. But how is that possible?

Let us look at the role of "imagination." Schopenhauer, who although among the last of the metaphysical-idealist thinkers about art (with his claim that artworks were not only graded objectifications of a metaphysical will but embodiments, in varying degrees of lucidity, of the Platonic Ideas), argued forcefully that imagination, or the creative insight of "genius," was the most objective form of consciousness. In contrast to fantasy makings, which satisfy only the wish-fulfilling needs of the ego, imaginative construction, he argued, when properly understood, is always imitative insofar as it discloses the essential character of reality, not simply as a symbol pointing to it but as a direct presentation of it.[17]

Aristotle defined *imagination* "as the ability to formulate, frame, and consider objects of sensation and cognition other than those directly anchored in the reality presented to the participant."[18] Francis Sparshott correctly notes that "The word 'fancy' comes from the Greek *phantasia*, which was used even in Latin as a sort of catch-all term for abilities and tendencies to envisage things as other than they are; the word 'imagination' was imported into the French and English languages at an early date from Latin, where as *imaginatio* it stood for various abilities and tendencies to manipulate or succumb to images and image-thinking, becoming especially popular as a technical term in rhetoric."[19]

"Imagination" is a large and compeling subject. Here, I want to draw philosophical attention to it only as it takes the form of "creative insight," neglecting thereby the traditional view that ties imagination to visualization or the having of mental images. Creative imagination, as I understand it, following Schopenhauer, is not an act of withdrawal from actuality; it is precisely an intensification and exploration of one's involvement with some one or more aspects or dimensions of reality. Imagination takes one outside one's little ego-based world by bringing the world into oneself. Creative imagination is an opening of the mind to reality: It is an act of appropriating experience and, through the appropriation, overcoming one's estrangement from it.

As noted by Schiller and others, imagination is a kind of play: It is a free creative activity. The creativity of nature as such, it is believed, is bound to governing laws and principles or to fortuitous happenings (random selection). Human creativity, on the other hand, is not "necessary" or "random." The process has causes and reasons, and it has limits (and indeed an artist often feels a certain necessity in that special need which creative expression can alone satisfy), but when genuine, the creativity is self-determining and thereby free. Although nature sets limits to any creative act (one cannot compose music in a range outside human aural perception), the artist acts spontaneously, with discipline, from the center of her being.

Imagination means a freedom from the seeing of things in terms of habituated responses and a freedom to create an ordered work.[20] Through imagination (which is always informed by intellect and a certain affectivity), one structures experience, one articulates new relationships between things, one brings forth objects of value, and thus by its very objective character it is bound to reality. Whenever imagination is free it enjoys an obedience to reality, being influenced by it, partaking of its essential character.

And, at the same time, it has its own subjective nature that is also reality oriented; for without memory, as Aristotle and Augustine knew, there is no imagination. This does not mean that if one were to suffer amnesia one would be unable to engage in artistic creativity; it means that an intensification of one's past experience made evident to consciousness as a presence pointing to the future is necessary for creativity in art. Imagination works in the (outer) present through the (inward) past directed to what is yet to be. It demands that one bring forth past intensities of experience, especially those that are rather useless for simply adapting to, or working in, the present and that one unite them with a vividly ordered content.

Creative imagination is thus always allied with insight or intuition and hence differs from mere "imaginings," with which it is so often confounded, just in this way—with daydreaming or a mere play of memories there is only the past or a wish-fulfilling future, with imagination there is a structuring in the present for the future through the intensities of the past. With daydreaming and the like, one is absorbed in oneself; with imagination one is outside of oneself through the appropriation of the past and the bringing forth of something that is new. With daydreaming one involuntarily roams the gamut of one's desires; with imagination one concentrates consciousness only on those relations that are to be structured.[21]

Creative imagination or artistic intuition, however, unlike pure spiritual intuition, does not demand a complete transcendence of the self. It is more an abandonment of the ego, a self-forgetfulness, in the intensity of a concentrated act than it is an utter self-surrender or self-denial. Its "content" is always at once phenomenal and noumenal, as it were, involving as it does a sensuous media and a silent spirituality—a power or rhythm of being (*ch'i-yun*, or "spirit resonance," as the traditional Chinese called it). Imagination in art does not take place independent of its expression, its embodiment in form. One does not have an artistic intuition into "spirit resonance" and then search around for a means of expressing it; rather, seeing and the expressing are, and appear, necessary to each other.

Without attempting to put forward a detailed psychology of imagination, one can, I think, confidently say that creative imagination is a kind of synthetic unity of intuition and representation. It is, we might say, an "intentional synthesis"; it aims to bring forth a presentation of reality.

Another way of putting this in more ordinary terms would be to say that creativity in art has always to do with working with a particular *medium*. (It is extraordinary how this is occasionally forgotten.) Imagination, creative insight, is carried out in and through the materials of the art form, and thus always involves intelligent or critical judgment. Recent analyses of creativity in art do take this into account but then, in their eagerness to rid themselves of any romantic vestiges, they err, it seems, in the other direction: They understand creativity to be just the exercise of this critical control, and they lack thereby any sense of the struggle, of the triumph, of the terrible or the joyful in creativity.[22] These analyses also err in neglecting the profound sense that the master artist has that one is more a *locus* than a *source* of the power of one's work, that one is the place where creative powers meet; in short, to use the old formulation, that one is an *instrument* of nature and not just a controller of a medium.[23]

Imitation in art, on the creative side, is thus a drawing from, which becomes a showing of, the power and rhythm of spiritual being and the presentation of reality. "Imitation" points the way to that "expression" in art which enables an artwork to be aesthetically forceful, its own meaning, and indeed to achieve the appropriate radiance and splendor of form that we see as the distinctive quality of that work of art that is beautiful.

3

Art Is Expression

Oil is "ex-pressed" from the olive; juice, from the grape. Traditional expression theories of art claim that an artist lets out his or her feelings and emotions in such a way that they are no longer simply turbulent, blind, and chaotic (as though that is what emotions are in the first place) but are ordered and clarified as they become embodied in the work of art and then cause or elicit an appropriate response or recognition in the experiencer of the work. "To express," according to the theory, is thus different from merely "to arouse" or "to exhibit" raw emotion, mainly by virtue of the lucidity or intelligibility that is said to be achieved by both the artist and the contemplative participant. Speaking of the actor's art, R. G. Collingwood, for example, writes:

> if his business is not amusement but art, the object at which he is aiming is not to produce a preconceived emotional effect on his audience but by means of a system of expressions, of language, composed partly of gesture, to explore his own emotions: to discover emotions in himself of which he was unaware, and, by permitting the audience to witness the discovery, enable them to make a similar discovery about themselves. In that case it is not her ability to weep real tears that would mark her out a good actress; it is her ability to make it clear to herself and her audience what her tears are about.

He goes on to say: "This applies to every kind of art. The artist never rants. A person who writes or paints or the like in order to blow off steam, using the traditional materials of art as means of exhibiting the symptoms of emotion, may deserve praise as an exhibitionist, but loses for the moment all claim to the title of artist."[1]

Most expressionist theory of art, as John Hospers has pointed out,[2] is confined to analyzing the expression of emotions or feelings; little is said about the artist's expression of ideas and concepts (although Tolstoy tends to combine the two when talking about the artist expressing the Christian idea of brotherhood). It is also based, as we have noted, primarily on a *causal* model of the relations that obtain between artist, artwork, and the experiencer of it. The model assumes that the artwork which results from the artist's expression of emotion is itself essentially a means to (cause of) a particular effect; namely, the experience of one who contemplates it.

But an artwork is an object of concentrated meaning and value. It is more a *source* than a cause; it is where aesthetic value is discerned. The feeling import of an artwork is in, or simply is, the artwork as much as any of its formal qualities. The artwork, I argue, does not so much cause or evoke or make for a simple recognition of an emotion (sadness, gaiety, or whatever); when properly responded to, it is recognized as having its own affective power as well as meaning and quality.

An artwork is the expression of emotion insofar as it presents a forceful aesthetic content that manifests the artist's successful transmutation of raw creative power into a controlled feeling that suffuses the work. *Imitation* refers to the participation in spiritual power, the grounding of creativity in reality; *expression* refers to the actual articulation of that power and its meaningful content by the created work of art.

The artist and the artwork, in this dimension, are thus as one. Criticisms of expression theory that want to leave the artist and his or her creativity completely out of the picture when judging a work of art (e.g., Hospers, "when we make a judgment of aesthetic value upon a work of art, we are in no way judging the process . . ."[3]) go to another extreme to avoid the naivete of the traditional theory, with its emphasis on the subjective or personal emotions of the artist. The creative process is one thing, the critics say; the work of art is something entirely different.

But, surely, a work of art is what it is by virtue of a particular creative process, the being of the artwork is its own becoming, if these terms may be allowed. The artwork, in short, is the process of its being: The brushwork is the painting or drawing as assuredly as its final color disposition. The aesthetic force of the painting, we might then say, is the power of its coming into being as controlled and disciplined and found, as it were, everywhere in the work. Lacking that power, artworks may be pretty and decorative, but they would fail to fulfill the intentionality of art itself, which aims to be powerful, meaningful, and beautiful.

Emotion in art is thus a kind of performance, so that the artwork itself may be said to be creative of the emotion that is presented and not simply expressive of an identifiable kind of life emotion.

Alasdair MacIntyre states that

> in different cultures the desires and emotions are organized differently and that there is therefore no single invariant human psychology. . . . Wants, satisfactions, and preferences never appear in human life as merely psychological, premoral items to which we can appeal as providing data that are neutral between rival moral claims. Why not?

> In every culture emotions and desires are norm-governed. Learning what the norms are, learning how to respond to the emotions and desires of others, and learning what to expect from others if we exhibit certain types and degrees of emotion or desire are three parts of one and the same task.[4]

We need then in the first place, I think, to distinguish in life emotionality between "raw emotive responses" and a full-fledged emotional state or act. I distinguish them as follows:

> A raw emotive response, in contrast to a full-fledged emotional act, is often based on identifiable "biologic" needs (e.g., the initial shock of fright one has at a loud, sudden, unexpected noise, the fright being traceable to primitive survival needs) and most often on what appears to be compelling "psychological" forces (e.g., the bursting into rage over some trivial affront, the outburst being accounted for in terms of repressed desires, or whatever). With raw responses we tend to look for causal explanations; with emotional states or acts we tend to look for rational justifications—and for the fitness of the response to its object. Raw emotional responses exhaust themselves; emotional acts strive to complete themselves. One is, with raw responses, very much their victim (the emotionality of the senile with its wayward anger and despair); with emotional states there is at the least a struggle to achieve a relative freedom through their understanding and appropriation.[5]

Raw emotive responses may, I believe, lay claim to a certain universality, rooted as they seem to be in various socio-biological conditions; emotional acts as such must, I think we have to agree with MacIntyre, be culture specific to a considerable extent in terms of the manner of their being "norm governed," albeit there may be instances of shared cross-cultural norms. Anyway, the idea that emotional states and acts are, in many ways, culture bound—there being no comprehensive universal set of definable emotional acts as such—does re-enforce the idea that emotion in art is a creative articulation of emotionality rather than an exhibition or an embodiment of a pre-existing condition.

Let us look briefly at two, quite different, non-western traditions that, I think, can help reorient our thinking about emotion in art.

Indian aesthetics developed a central concept, *rasa*, which is applied to a wide range of experience and creative expression. The concept was first codified by Bharata (second–fifth? centuries) and was given its fullest elaboration in the tenth century by the Kashmiri philosopher Abhinavagupta. The term *rasa* literally means "flavor" and in the aesthetic context means that which is "tasted" in art. The realization of this essential quality of aesthetic experience, according to the theory, requires that the content of art is never (or at least ought never to be) just the personal emotions or thoughts of either the artist or the experiencer. M. Hiriyanna, a twentieth century philosopher and historian of Indian philosophy, rightfully points out that "the poet's own feeling, according to the

Rasa view, is *never* the theme of poetry."[6] It is, then, precisely this impersonality (*sādhāraṇikaraṇa*) of aesthetic content that enables the artwork to serve as a bearer of meaning and the experiencer to rise to a heightened consciousness of self and world. As a generalized emotion, the *rasa*, however, is not, according to the theory, to be confounded with a mere abstract or utterly dispassionate state of being. To depersonalize does not destroy the personal but allows for its transformation. How is this possible?

According to the psychology underlying the theory, experience is an awakening or manifestation of various innate states (*bhāvas*), such as delight (*rati*), humor (*hāsa*), pain (*śōka*), which exist in the mind (or "heart") as latent impressions (*saṃskāras* or *vāsanās*) that derive from one's past experience. Each *bhāva* is said to be accompanied by causes, which are understood to be the various situations and events of life that occasion an appropriate response, by effects, the various visible behavior (gestures, facial expressions), and by concomitant elements, the various accompanying but temporary mental states such as anxiety. According to the theory, when these aspects of ordinary experience become features of art and aesthetic experience they are called, respectively, *determinants* (*vibhāva*), the emotional situation that is presented say in a drama; *consequents* (*anubhāva*), the physical changes or movements that signify emotional states; and *transitory states* (*vyabhicāribhāva*), the transient emotions that properly accompany various basic states.

Aesthetic experience, for the *rasa* theory, therefore, is essentially a "relishing" of certain generalized emotions that are objectified and transformed in the artwork. Although an artwork that occasions a *rasa* is closely related to common affective experience, drawing as it does its own vitality from those basic life emotions, it nevertheless always creates its own unique emotionality. "The tasting of Rasa," Abhinavagupta writes, ". . . differs from both memory, inference and any form of ordinary self-consciousness."[7] For the *rasa* theory, then, the dominant emotion of an artwork, the poem, the play is closely related to the work's own feeling-tone and, in fact, may be said to dictate that tonality. V. K. Chari, who, in his interesting work *Sanskrit Criticism*, expounds the theory in great detail and argues for its universality, writes: "if one emotional pattern is exhibited over and over again and is echoed and reechoed in all parts of the work, that pattern would then become the dominant theme and dictate the tone of the entire work. . . . The *rasa* chosen to be the dominant mood of the poem spreads itself as a pervasive quality of the work through all its parts."[8] Now insofar as every successful artwork, according to this Indian theory, has a dominant *rasa*, it would follow that a work's feeling-tone is always and necessarily coincident with its *rasa* and could not therefore ever be contradictory to it.

* * *

According to Zeami (1363–1443), who, it is often said, perfected the Nō theater of Japan in its classic form and brought it to its highest level,[9] "the mark of supreme attainment in all of the arts and accomplishments"[10] is *yūgen*. *Yūgen* has been defined as *charme subtile* (*"Je précise que ce n'est pas là une traduction exacte de yūgen: cette interprétation m'a été suggérée par le contexte, et confirmée par mon expérience personnelle du nō"*);[11] as that "supreme form of beauty . . . which is the ultimate goal and the essential element of all aesthetic experience";[12] and as "the beauty not merely of appearance but of the spirit; it is inner beauty manifesting itself outward."[13]

Peter Lamargue, in his highly interesting work on Nō, states and asks:

> On the face of it there are two irreconcilable requirements of a Noh actor (in the central, or *shite*, role). One is that he should bring alive the character he is portraying, breathing into the part both spirit and expression. The other is that he should conform unwaveringly to the strict conventions of the role, under which every gesture and intonation are prescribed; his own facial expressions are concealed behind a mask; the words he chants and intones are passages of dense, allusive poetry; his dance movements are symbolic and ritualistic; there are virtually no props on the bare stage; and the character he portrays—an old woman, a warrior, a god—appears insubstantial, even stereotypical. What room is there for expressiveness behind this mask of formality?[14]

He answers: "The characters are *abstract* to a high degree; their constitutive attributes are *impersonal*, albeit retaining some individuality; and they seek to embody *universal*, rather than historical or contingent, significance. . . . The portrayal emphasizes emotion rather than motivation; inner spirit rather than action; mood rather than factual detail; and suggestion rather than realistic representation."[15]

Let us concentrate here on the emotion dimension. Lamarque goes on to state that: "Attention is directed to a purified and intensified emotion, unmediated by mere contingency of personality."[16] The aim "is to offer, or attempt to offer, direct access to the inner phenomenology of an emotion by somehow embodying it in the actor's performance."[17] And, when it is rightfully embodied through the actor's complete identification with what is expressed, *yūgen* shines forth.

Another way of understanding this is through the concept of *monomane*, literally "imitation," but of a very special kind closely related to how I have previously interpreted it. For Zeami, "it crucially involves the imitation of inner spirit, i.e., a hidden essence, not (or not merely) outward mannerism or appearance."[18] Thus, "For any part involving *monomane* an actor must learn to truly 'become' the object of his performance."[19]

For Zeami, then, the artist is called on not to copy or mimic outward sensible objects or actions or nature's productive activity or a principle (*li*) that is thought to constitute the essential form or structure of things (Confucian *wen-jen* theory); rather he must articulate a dynamic symbol, becoming in fact that which is symbolized. The situation depicted must resound with associations drawn both from life experience and from story and legend but must stand always as a concentrated presentation of a particular emotion to be found nowhere else but in the action presented.

Both Bharata's *rasa* theory in its relation to classical Sanskrit drama and Zeami's prescriptions for Nō stress the articulation of emotion in highly stylized, conventional ways (as opposed to its mere exhibition). Emotion in art, for them, is tied to, that is, has direct reference to, life emotion but radically displaces, as it were, that life experience when presented as an articulated form. The emotion whose essence is revealed to us is no longer an episodic state of a particular person, explainable or describable by reference to a determined set of causes or reasons, motivations, or desires but that which, through the remarkable identifying power and skill of the master actor and the sensitive discernment of the viewer comes to belong to the actor and the viewer as a universal possibility. The art emotion becomes then sui generis; it is precisely what is created in its performance.[20] Let us explore this further in our own terms.

* * *

When, for example, we say that Mahler's *Kindertotenlieder* is "sad" or expresses "sadness," we do not mean that it elicit sadness in us—those who respond aesthetically to it. There is, it seems, no correlation between an expressive property of a musical work and what it may call forth in its auditors. When we say, then, that Mahler's music expresses sadness, we mean, I propose, that first of all we recognize an overall emotional quality present in the music (formally in terms primarily of its pace and tonality) by analogy with our life emotionality and respond aesthetically to it as we further recognize and come to appreciate it as it stands in its own integrity as the unique, particular concentration of feeling that it is.

If we look at the various terms a critic might use to describe tonalities in art we would certainly count among them *forceful, precious, somber, tender, vibrant, insipid, gentle*—terms that, although borrowed as it were from ordinary experience, intend to point to a unifying affective quality in the work that has special aesthetic significance. For better or worse, we translate that unique aesthetic quality, when appropriate, into the language of emotionality, saying that the work exhibits (some, of course, say evokes) "power," "fear," "loathing," "anger," and the rest. But this language, as with the language of tonality itself, in virtue of its generality, disguises what in fact we are saying or intending to say about what we discern to be present uniquely in the particular work. The work creates its own feeling; it does not refer as such to episodic, occurrent emotional states of a kind with which we are familiar in our life experiences.

What distinguishes art emotion from life emotion is, among other things, the lack of a belief-based cognitivity in art emotion. Life emotions, it is often argued, involve judgments about certain states of affairs (about that which occasions the emotion), about, in fact, precisely what that state of affairs is—and we look in life emotions for a certain proportionality between the nature of the particular situation that occasions the emotion and the intensity of the belief-induced response to it. We do not, on the other hand, regard art emotions as involving judgmental factors about specific states of affairs; they stand, rather—insofar as they are an integral part of the work's aesthetic content as distinct from its subject matter as such—in their own complete affective integrity. Their "proportionality" is purely aesthetic, internal to the work and not a measure of some kind between the work and a situation external to it.[21]

Edvard Munch's well-known "expressionistic" work *The Cry* (1893) is about terror and anxiety: That is its subject matter and at the same time it shows what it means to be terrified—"*The Cry* is an agonized shriek translated into visible vibrations that spread out like Art Nouveau sound waves"[22]—by way of (to use Nelson Goodman's terms) its "metaphorical exemplification," and may, for all we know, exhibit something about Munch's own attitudes toward, or concerns about, the life phenomenon referred to. But what it presents aesthetically as its content is the special feeling-tone embedded in what is represented that refers us to no particular life situation or indeed to a specifiable individual as such. The tense tonality simply is in and of the work itself.

The very paucity of the language we employ in designating feelings and emotions in art reflects our awareness of the unique, nonrepeatable character of those feelings. If each successful work of art performs its own emotionality, it is not at all surprising that the viewer, the critic, indeed the artist have difficulty in labeling it: The understanding of it and the experience of it are not two different things.

* * *

When a discrepancy is evident between an isolable content in art (a conventional symbolic meaning, literal reference, or message) and a sensuous form that adorns the message or meaning to ease its communication, we have either propaganda (a disguised sociology, politics, etc.) or simply bad didactic art. In a genuine or successful artwork, "expression" constitutes the aesthetic and irreducible meaning of the work; it does not convey a separate meaning—or symbol of emotion.

Following Susanne K. Langer, we can, I think, properly say that an artwork is an expressive form—but only as it is creative of the meaning that is expressed. Langer is surely correct, then, in noting that an artwork

> is a symbol in a somewhat special sense, because it performs some symbolic functions, but not all; especially it does not stand for something else, nor refer to anything that exists apart from it. According to the usual definition of 'symbol,' a work of art should not be classed as a symbol at all. But that usual definition [of something standing for something else] overlooks the greatest

> intellectual value and, I think, the prime office of symbols—their power of formulating experience, and presenting it objectively for contemplation, logical intuition, recognition, understanding.[23]

Another way of putting this would be to say that when art achieves autonomy its meaning is no longer to be found merely in a set of conventional symbols or in a series of independently formulated concepts, rather its meaning becomes inherent in it. The meaning of an artwork is its aesthetic content. The work may have a recognizable subject matter (although this is seldom the case with music or architecture), and the subject matter (constituted by familiar images, representations, or graphic symbols of whatever sort) may contribute to the work's meaning; but the meaning is not reducible to the associations that gather about the symbols or about the referential elements themselves. "Meaning" in art becomes then a realization of the possibilities of the artwork itself. *A work of art is meaningful to the degree to which it realizes the possibilities that it itself gives rise to.*

The chief difficulty that one has in articulating the special inherent meaning of an artwork is to be found in our general theoretical dependence on the notion that meaning = referentiality (in some sense or other), that—despite the "deconstructionist" program—"projected referential meaning" has primacy (if not exclusivity) for meaning in general. Leonard Meyer, for example, accepts a definition of *meaning* as " 'anything acquires meaning if it is connected with, or indicates, or refers to something beyond itself, so that its full nature points to and is revealed in that connection' " and concludes that "Meaning is thus not a property of things. It cannot be located in the stimulus alone. The stimulus may have different meanings. To a geologist a large rock may indicate that at one time a glacier began to recede at a given spot; to a farmer the same rock may point to the necessity of having the field cleared for plowing; and to the sculptor the rock may indicate the possibility of artistic creation. A rock, a word, or motion in and of itself, merely as a stimulus, is meaningless."[24]

But a work of art is not a rock or just a neutral stimulus. Works of art are precisely unlike natural objects in having their own meaning, in realizing their own possibilities independent of any particular mode of selective perception. A work of art may, of course, be perceived extra-aesthetically—by an art dealer as an object of potential profit, by a mover as something to be crated carefully and handled gently, and so on. Aesthetically, however, the work of art has (and is) an intrinsic meaning—its realization of the possibilities that it itself gives rise to.

But what does it mean "to realize possibilities"? For an artwork, *realization*, I would argue means the bringing of the work to an appropriate conclusion and exhibiting the process by which that conclusion is achieved.

Works of art are, as it were, purposive forms, which is to say that once initiated they strive to fulfill ends appropriate to them. Octavio Paz writes: "The poem flows, marches. And that flowing is what gives it unity. Now, to flow not only means to move but to move toward something; the tension that inhabits words and hurtles them forward is going to the encounter of something. Words seek a word that will give meaning to their march, stability to their mobility."[25] And Susanne K. Langer notes, with respect to drama, that

> Before a play has progressed by many lines, one is aware not only of vague conditions of life in general, but of a special situation. Like the distribution of figures on a chessboard, the combination of characters makes a strategic pattern. . . . Where in the real world we would witness some extraordinary act and gradually understand the circumstances that lie behind it, in the theatre we perceive an ominous situation and see that some far-reaching action must grow out of it. This creates the peculiar tension between the given present and its yet unrealized consequent, "form in suspense," the essential dramatic illusion.[26]

The poem, the play, as indeed the painting and the musical composition creates its own conditions of expectation, prediction, and anticipation that call for (some kind of) resolution and fulfillment. This "process of completion" requires that the viewer not only apprehend what is actually realized, but that she have a sense of the way in which the appropriate, informing selections are made. When experiencing a painting, for example, one is called upon to see it not only as a finished thing, as something static, but as a dynamic "resoluting" of various tensions and contrasts as they develop integrally in the work as it seeks its right fulfillment. And the progress toward fulfillment—the process that is exhibited—is not, of course, mechanical; it is not a matter of the artist setting down initial words, colors, lines, spaces, or sounds and then having everything else inevitably follow from this setting down, as conclusions might from premises in a deductive argument, for the "appropriateness" of a conclusion or consummation of the work depends as well on elements of novelty and surprise. Also, a work of art defines itself not only in the sense of the artist's selection of elements, with initial selections influencing, but not determining, what consequently occurs, but also, as we have seen, in the full affective sense of its establishing its own special and appropriate tone, its own unique and right articulation of feeling.

But what, then, is the import of that which essentially creates and is its own meaning? "Intuition," once again, we have suggested, has primarily to do with the influence of reality on the artwork, the manner in which, through the objectivity of creative consciousness, the aesthetic content is informed by reality. "Expression," we now suggest, has to do with the manifest presence of formal relationships that constitute the work, relationships that, imbued with feeling, derive their significance from their own inherent rightness. This is, in a way, circular; but it is a circularity that is inevitable and is itself revealing of the uniqueness of meaning (a meaning that does not merely stand for something else or that is merely associative; i.e., gathered about a particular subject matter) that is present in any successful work of art. It is the particular way in which an individual work of art presents itself as suffused with feeling in and through its own aesthetic content, which makes it count as an expressive form—and sometimes as a radiant form.

* * *

Beauty in art, we have come to believe, largely through the achievements of modern art, is not reducible to the "attractive," to the "pretty," or to what might answer to any simple formula for "perfection." Beauty rather has to do with aesthetic authenticity, with what is right for the individual, particular work of art as an aesthetic presence or expressive form. The beauty of an artwork is thus inseparable from its aesthetic force and meaningful content. It is the artwork itself as a radiant form.

Beauty in nature, unlike in art, is the mere play of various sensuous qualities—light, shadows, gathering clouds, rising mountains—in their own random/determinative distribution. Unless one were a radical theist, seeing everything that happens in nature as the work of a divine presence, that presence then being the artist of a sunset, we tend to see beauty in nature as a transient, contingent quality of various elements in relation to one another. We tend to see the beauty of the scene as fortuitous, knowing nevertheless that it is the result or product, as we have noted, of indifferent natural forces. In art, on the other hand, there is only meaningful or expressive beauty. Let me explain.

Classical "objectivist" positions have held, as Anthony Savile notes, that "attributions of beauty are true or false according as the designated object does or does not have the property ascribed to it. Our response of pleasure or love is rooted in the object, but that response is not constitutive of the object's beauty, rather its beauty explains the response."[27]

Savile then states that this "realist" view could not meet the challenge of having "to explain how there can always be an informative answer to the question, What makes this object beautiful?"[28] And thus we are led to the opposite position, which casts the subjectivity of the viewer in center stage, culminating in Kant's opening assertion in his *Critique of Judgment* that "If we wish to distinguish whether anything is beautiful or not we do not refer the representation of it to the object . . . but to the subject and its feeling of pleasure and pain"[29] and in Santanaya's claim in *The Sense of Beauty* that beauty is but "objectified pleasure."

But does a "nonsubjectivist" understanding of "beauty" actually require that one explain what makes all objects beautiful by reference to a specified feature or set of features that they must possess? Many efforts have, of course, been made to do just that by way of an appeal to "harmony," "organic unity," and the like, but they perhaps have been wrongheaded in accepting the subjectivist's challenge in the first place, for their answers do presuppose that beauty is precisely a property of an object and not the object itself as presented and responded to in a certain way.

Indeed the history of the opposition between those who thought beauty could be determined as some objective feature of the object perceived and those who, despairing of ever finding such a feature or set of them, claimed that beauty resided in some essential way in the subjective response of its beholder lends credence to the possibility that the whole problem was framed wrongly in its assumption that beauty is a property of an object and not the object itself as *shown* rightly.

Guy Sircello, who has written the most in recent times on the concept of beauty develops what he calls a *fragmentarian* view of beauty, which he sets up in opposition to various *unitarian* views. "The unitarian impulse," he writes, "has manifested itself in several different ways. Perhaps the most important of these has been the emphasis on beauty as 'wholeness.' . . . To embody the theme of wholeness, a theory must allege or imply that that which is beautiful is so precisely insofar as its parts exhibit some specific kind of unity." Integral to his "fragmentarian" view, on the other hand, is that of a "partitive principle," which "invites us to see the beauty of each thing as merely a 'part' of that thing" and hence "that not only do beautiful things have beauty as parts of themselves, but they might have many different beauties as parts of themselves."[30]

But our apprehension of beauty seems to give rise to our noticing and attending more closely to the features and qualities of the work that make for its rightness, rather than the other way around. In aesthetic perception (and this is probably the case as well for all perception), we do not first see (and examine) isolable parts and pieces and then pronounce their totality to be right or wrong; rather, we move from an initial gestalt apprehension to particular elements and then back and forth, the apprehension being deepened and enriched by that hermeneutical play. In short, many different things and sorts of things—and even "parts" of things when they are taken as gestalts—can indeed be beautiful and in varied ways with the concept "beauty" nevertheless being the principle of radiant rightness of the object itself.

Beauty in art *is*, then, when form or aesthetic content radiates, which is to say, when the artwork itself exhibits as a whole a fulfilling rightness, one that is suffused with a feeling appropriate to it. A work of art simply lacks beauty when it fails to exhibit that rightness and not when it presents, say, expressionistic disfigurement, conflicting color relations, disproportions, and the like, many of which may contribute to the particular work's rightness and even bring about alterations in a culture's criteria or "standard" of the beautiful.[31]

The opposite of beauty in art is not ugliness but a kind of nullity or unrealized intentionality.

The beauty of an artwork is thus always "objective" insofar as the work itself as object shows itself as a radiant form and is right for itself. Beauty in art is not something superadded to the work, rather it is throughout constitutive of it. If beauty were absent, the object would simply fail as an artwork; it would become its given thinghood. Beauty in art, one might then say, is irresistible; it compels us toward the work in the fullness of its presence.

Beauty, as so understood, is as central a feature of the intentionality of art as its drive to be aesthetically powerful and meaningful. An artwork expresses beauty, then, just as the expressive form that it is, which is to say once again, that its process, its being brought into presentational form by human creativity, and its presence are inseparable. When we radically sunder artist from artwork and artwork from a contemplative participant who has adopted a certain aesthetic attitude of detachment, we fail to recognize the special intentionality of art to be powerful, meaningful, and beautiful. This intentionality, when fulfilled, is integral to the artwork. The aesthetic quality of an artwork, in short is not an isolable formal arrangement any more than its meaning is an isolable symbolic content. To experience an artwork as an expressive form requires, then, the full play of one's intellectual and intuitive as well as one's sensuous powers of discernment.

4

Aesthetic Experience and the Artwork

I have argued that, to formulate a right conception of art, one must not radically sunder the artist from the artwork and the artwork from the contemplative participant of it.[1] An artwork is what it is in virtue of a "creative process," which process (of intellect, feeling, intuition) enables an artwork to be at once imitative and expressive and to fulfill its intentionality to be aesthetically forceful, significant, and beautiful. At the same time, the artwork has its being, as it were, in a world of consciousness (it *is* as an artwork rather than just an object or thing only for consciousness) and hence as such it cannot be conceived as completely independent of the experience of it.[2]

Aesthetic experience has often been reduced to or analyzed exclusively in terms of either an aesthetic attitude (of disinterestedness, detachment) or an aesthetic emotion (of refined pleasure). Since Kant, at least, it has become commonplace to oppose an aesthetic attitude to a practical one. An aesthetic attitude, it is said, exists for its own sake; the object of perception is not, as with a practical attitude taken as a means to some further end but is approached as an end in itself, worthy of our close attention (Jerome Stolnitz). In aesthetic experience we must disengage any personal or utilitarian interests we might otherwise have in the object in favor of attending exclusively to its intrinsic qualities. We must, it is said, be detached so that we may be open to what is presented by the artwork. An appropriate "distance" must be interposed between ourselves and the artwork in order that we may experience the artwork aesthetically.[3]

Now, however the aesthetic attitude is to be defined, it is evident that this attitude (basically of our openness to the work) is not itself the essential character of aesthetic experience; rather it is a *condition* for that experience. Before one can relate to an artwork (or to a natural object) as an aesthetic object one must suspend one's practical and other inhibiting interests in it. This suspension is necessary for the apprehension of the aesthetic qualities of the object, but it is surely not sufficient for our experiencing the work of art rightly in the fullness of its being. A proper "aesthetic attitude," in short, might enable us to experience an artwork properly, but the attitude is not the basic nature of the experience itself.

Clive Bell has argued that "all sensitive people agree that there is a peculiar emotion provoked by works of art" and that "we have no other means of recognizing a work of art than our feeling for it."[4] Now, whether this "aesthetic emotion" is ours as such or is "objectified" as pleasure in the artwork (Santayana), it is clear, as I have argued, that this emotion is also not the essential character of our experience of artworks, for it does not take into account the special cognitive and spiritual dimensions of the experience. The "aesthetic emotion" needs to be seen as integral to a deeper and more complex experiential unity.

The experience of an artwork (which is aesthetically forceful, meaningful, and beautiful) involves, I believe, *assimilation*, *recognition*, and *discernment* and calls for a special *appropriation* that yields an integrated wholeness. Let me explain.

In actual life, when we meet a situation of power or force (especially of violence), we react to it, we protect ourselves from it, we might even act forcefully in turn. With works of art, on the other hand, we assimilate the aesthetic force; we take it on, as it were, as a condition of our own being; we incorporate it into our emotional texture and freely accept it. Assimilation is a kind of empathetic embrace, but it is not an attributing of a psychophysiological process to a particular shape or configuration (Vernon Lee's "mountain rising"); it is rather an *awakening* of our feeling to what is presented by the artwork. Our being is influenced by the work, as the work, through the artist, was itself influenced by a power and rhythm of being.

The aesthetic force of an artwork, in short,—when the work is right—does not just overwhelm the experiencer of it; rather, although it might appear initially alien to one, it is presented as an opportunity for one's intimate and transformative relationship with it.

We assimilate aesthetic force. We *recognize* meaning. In aesthetic experience the inherent significance of the artwork presents itself to us as something to be recognized rather than as something to be known conceptually. Recognition is, of course, a kind of knowing; it has own noetic character, but it differs from conceptual knowing, discursive understanding, and abstract, rational thought by virtue of its immediacy and qualitative discrimination. To *recognize* means to *apprehend*: It means to see mentally that a work has realized possibilities that it itself has given rise to, that the work has been brought to an appropriate conclusion and is exhibiting the process by which that conclusion was achieved.

Recognition of this type presupposes, therefore, a keen sensitivity and a knowledgeable background. One is called upon to recognize novelty and originality and at the same time to take in thematic and other purely symbolic achievements, as well as affective tones; one is called upon, in short, to apprehend the full range of meaning that constitutes the work.

Meaning is the locus for the cognitive in art. In our experience of artworks we must be knowing participants. We are not called upon to know what the work "means" but to apprehend that meaning as it is the work.

We assimilate aesthetic force; we recognize inherent significance or meaning; we *discern* that the work is rightly beautiful. Aesthetic experience, on its formal side or in its formal dimension, is not just a noticing of qualities and a passing over the qualities to other aspects that interest one, as is the case generally with ordinary perception; it is precisely a close attentiveness to the play of colors, lines, shapes, sounds, spaces, and rhythms as they at once have their own integrity and contribute to the work as a formal gestalt. Discernment means discrimination and judgment; it is an activity of the experiencer; it is an active engagement between a work and the contemplative participant of it.

Now, assimilation, recognition, and discernment are not, in actuality, separate moments or features of experience; rather they interfuse, intermingle, and together are the *process* of our relating to works of art. The process does require the full play of one's intellectual and intuitive as well as sensuous powers and, under the control of the artwork, may bring about an integration and wholeness to the experiencer of the work. And just as the creative process that brings the artwork into being is at the same time a self-articulation and self-formation of the artist, so this play of the experiencer's powers is a kind of self-appropriation—the realization of the self's own spirituality. Spirit meets spirit in art—and an integrated wholeness, however temporary or enduring, is achieved.

5

Summary Definition of a Work of Art

A work of art, even though culturally embedded, thus has its own intentionality, which is precisely its aiming to be aesthetically forceful, meaningful, and beautiful.

A work of art is aesthetically forceful to the degree to which it manifests an immanent spiritual power, which power or rhythm of being is everywhere present in the work and is discerned as a unique vitality.

A work of art is inherently significant, is meaningful, to the degree to which it realizes the possibilities that it itself gives rise to; realization being a bringing of the work to a right conclusion and an exhibiting of the process by which the right conclusion is reached.

A work of art is beautiful to the degree to which it presents as its own presence a formal achievement, a radiance and splendor of form, that is appropriate to it.

A work of art is an object for consciousness and is experienced by assimilation (of its aesthetic force), recognition (of its inherent meaning), and discernment (of its beauty); the three together forming a single process of experience that culminates in a self-appropriation or realization of the self's own spirituality.

A work of art is thus that created object which, when realizing its own intentionality, is at once imitative and expressive and performs, for consciousness, its own aesthetic content.

Part II

6

Temporality and the Visual Arts

Aestheticans today seldom speak, as did Lessing in the eighteenth century in his famous *Laocoön*, of a sharp division in the arts between "the spatial" and "the temporal"; nevertheless there remains a widespread belief that, unlike music and drama where time seems to be part of their very substance, painting, sculpture, drawing have temporal significance only in a secondary, derivative or marginal way. However, it seems quite evident, a number of temporal dimensions in the visual arts are, or may be in different individual works, of considerable aesthetic importance and need to be carefully distinguished and discerned. Let us regard Paul Klee's *Heavenly and Earthly Time*.

The work was completed in 1927. Like all other constructed things, it is datable: The work came into and retains its being in a public, measured, indifferent time. Also, it can be experienced only within a duration of public time; which is to say, there is the successive moments that it takes to experience the work, a time that varies, of course, with each person and with the same person at different times and places, albeit the work itself sets a "normal range", if you will, for the experience of it.[1]

These temporal aspects of the datability of the work and the duration required for its apprehension are not of any special significance for the visual arts, as they obviously apply as well to many other kinds of aesthetic and nonaesthetic experience. One other aspect of this public, measured time, though, requires special acknowledgment, that is the effect of "temporal passage" on the work itself, both physically and conceptually. As a physical object, a work of visual art is subject to change due to the nature of the materials used, to deterioration (especially with frescoes), in virtue of the varied effects of the environment upon it (from that of natural light to pollution in the air). Some artists, especially architects, are able to anticipate some of these changes (e.g., the weathering effect on certain woods, the alterations in color due to the chemical nature of the pigments), other changes simply occur at time's mercy, the work being helpless to avoid uncalled-for physical transformations.

Figure 6.1. Paul Klee (Swiss 1879–1940). *Heavenly and Earthly Time*, 1927. Watercolor and ink on paper. 9 5/8 x 12 inches. '50-134-117 Philadelphia Museum of Art: The Louise and Walter Arensberg Collection

The visual work insofar as it is representational and not purely abstract (but even then what is understood to be "abstract" may vary from time to time) is always subject as well to the historicity of interpretation, to its being situated in what phenomenologists are fond of calling *lived history* (as opposed to mere chronology), which can render its subject matter alive, as it were, or dead. One could well imagine a not-distant future when the notion of "heavenly time" was simply unintelligible as a possible valid ontological concept.

A work of art, we have said before, is not just a static completion, but rather embodies its own dynamic process of coming into being. In short, an artwork exhibits the temporality of its making. We sense this in Klee's work through the continuities and the discontinuities of its lines, the careful but not rigidly determined directionalities, in the various markings and shadings of light and dark—the chiaroscuro—and so on. We experience the work as an embodied creative process.

And we also, in our example of Klee's work, experience the work as it is itself *about* time—about a human-ordered temporality and the distant still-point of eternity, and the tense relations between them. The church tower with its clock as the intersection between busy extended events and the precarious balance of the suspended forces—the whole visual presentation being like a frozen mobile ready to move with the slightest disturbance—tells us something about what time means and is for us. Now, of course, not all works of visual art are about time in the explicit fashion of Klee's *Heavenly and Earthly Time*; however, many works do employ various symbols and other visual devices that clearly express temporal meanings—transitoriness, aging, seasonal cycles—and sometimes larger philosophic attitudes toward what time and history themselves are. So long as human life is an organic process and not simply a duration measured in terms of a succession of indifferent moments, temporal representations will be an important thematic concern of visual art, for it has its own special powers to explore and articulate that concern.

Writing about the difficulties we have in arriving "at a conception of a whole which is constructed from parts belonging to different dimensions,"[2] Paul Klee states that "To each dimension, as, with the flight of time, it disappears from view, we should say: now you are becoming the Past. But possibly later at a critical—perhaps fortunate—moment we may meet again on a new dimension, and once again you may become the Present."[3]

A work of visual art, like a musical work, is creative of a formal temporality that exists nowhere else but in the work. This is the inherent rhythm, the dynamic play exhibited in the relations of its elements. It is a *virtual* temporal order constructed by the artist formally in and through the tempo and phrasing of the work. It is no accident that the language of music is employed here as well, for just as music paradigmatically is creative of its own formal temporality, so, although in a much less transparent way, the visual arts set forth temporal relations of their own making through their controlling of color contrasts, background and foreground shiftings, arrangements of objects, and so on. Mikel Dufrenne notes that "harmony is the principle of movement in painting—just as it is in music, where sensuous qualities need a keynote and whose dissonance calls for a chord of resolution. Such movement is ordered by rhythm and thus manifests a duration which is born of the animation of space."[4]

Here, the concept of "timing" is of the utmost importance, for what gives aesthetic value to the temporalities created in the work is precisely their achieving a rightness appropriate to them, a rightness we perceive qualitatively as right timing—the creating of temporal relations that belong together, however tension laden they may be. Like with the unfolding of events in a novel where, when the narrative is right, there seems to be an inevitability in the pattern presented, so with a painting, a drawing, we have the subtle bringing together of visual happenings that become constitutive of the form perceived.

Time, then, is performed in the visual arts as much, though in very different and more elusive ways, as in any of the "temporal arts."

7

Mallarmé and Valéry and the Essence of Poetry

> La poésie est l'expression, par le langage humain ramené à son rythme essentiel, du sense mystérieux des aspects de l'existence: elle doue ainsi d'authenticité notre séjour et *constitue* la seule tâche spirituelle.
>
> (Mallarmé)

One of the most remarkable characteristics of an artist is his or her ability to discover limitless possibilities for creativity and to carry one such possibility to its furthest limit. It is as if the artist were able to know herself and her art only through extremes, only through isolating some one possibility of her nature and her art and taking it as far as it can go.

The "pure poets" Stéphane Mallarmé and Paul Valéry attempted to take poetic creativity and the poem to what is certainly just such an extreme, and although they were doomed to fail in their enterprise, their efforts, I believe, did disclose something about the essential nature of poetry.[1]

* * *

Building on the work of Gautier, Baudelaire, and Poe, Mallarmé and Valéry sought to make of poetry something sacred and timeless. A purity formed by the sound, the rhythm, and the noncognitive suggestiveness of words alone was to radiate from and constitute the poem.

> What is "form" for anyone else is "content" for me.
>
> Out of a number of words, poetry fashions a single new word which is total in itself and foreign to the language—a kind of incantation.[3]
>
> If the poem is to be pure, the poet's voice must be stilled and the initiative taken by the words themselves, which will be set in motion as they meet unequally in collision.[4]

> Literature exists first of all as a way of developing our powers of invention and self-stimulation in the utmost freedom, since its matter and tool is the *word*, freed from the burden of immediate use.[5]

These very typical quotations from Mallarmé and Valéry indicate that the "pure poet" is one who imposes a kind of artificial alienation upon himself for the sake of dissociating the medium of poetry, "the word," from the ordinary worlds of human experience. The word is to be a symbol symbolizing only itself. A poem is to subsist in a unique realm of perfection. "The meaning of a poetic work," according to Wallace Fowlie's reading of Mallarmé, "is inseparable from its structure. The language of a poem, which cannot be changed or paraphrased, is its meaning. The words of a poem, their sequence and their rhythm, are absolute. To modify them or to substitute other words for them, is to break their spell. A ritual is valid only when it is performed exactly and integrally."[6]

The conception of creativity as a ritual—as a sacred rite that, to be effective, must be performed with exactitude—is at the heart of the pure poet's work. Although Mallarmé and Valéry are among the most sophisticated of modern poets, a kind of word magic, if not language superstition, underlies their identification of poetic power with linguistic purity: there is something "primitive" in their investing language with a holy power.

But, unlike the primitive, Mallarmé and Valéry thought language could be created ex nihilo. No primal sounds like the great *akṣara* (syllable) of early Brahmanic thought (*Om*), from which all sounds originate, exist for them, and neither is there a pre-existing world of experience that demands their creative ordering. The poet is a creator of the biblical rather than of the Platonic or Neoplatonic variety. One *creates* a poem; one does not demiurgically form existing materials.

The making of *la poésie pure* becomes then a kind of cosmic as well as personal rite. But poetry is not merely akin to religion in this formalistic, ritualistic sense, as it is to replace religion entirely. The creation of a poem ex nihilo, and the aesthetic experience of it, is able, it is believed, to encompass all the cognitive insights and emotional responses traditionally associated with religion. But, whereas religious language and ritual act are understood (by many theologians, historians of religion, and enlightened practitioners) to be essentially symbolic, pointing beyond themselves to something else, poetic language and the creative act are to be utterly autonomous; they are to require nothing outside of themselves.

Language is therefore to be divested of all didacticism so that it may yield a pure musical response. "Every name is a symbol," as Fowlie also notes for Mallarmé, "and generates other symbols. . . . They attain an autonomous life and meaning of their own, and hence a purity similar . . . to any art whose beauty seems to come solely from its own symbols and to remain independent of the experience which preceded its form in art."[7] But as Valéry was later to admit, a pure poem (and especially the act of bringing it forth) is, if not impossible, at the very borderline that separates the possible from the impossible. "Just as the perfect void . . . cannot be attained, cannot even be approached except at the price of an exhausting succession of efforts, so," Valéry writes, "the ultimate purity of our art, for those who have such a conception of it, demands such endless and rude restraints that they absorb all the natural joy in being a poet and, in the end, leave him nothing but the pride of never being satisfied."[8] The pure poet, in short, wants his poem "to be" and at the same time to be free from all the contents of relational experience which customarily give linguistic expression its reason for being.

And this is carried over from verse to the expression of prosaic ideas themselves. "My early, and very short practice of the art of verse," Valéry writes, " had accustomed me to making use of words, and even 'ideas,' as means which have only passing values and are effective only by the reason of their placing."[9] Rather than ideas being a function of our relations with the world and with other persons, their value is to be derived solely from their placing in a literary context. In its extreme form this would imply that the rhythm, the tone, the form in which an idea is expressed becomes—and not just contributes to—the meaning of the idea. The pure writer, then, in this extreme form of his program for language, would turn completely upside down any kind of pragmatist or empiricist criterion of meaning. Ideas are neither to be acted upon (or, if so, only incidentally) nor are they to be verified in experience. An idea is exhausted by the aesthetic manner in which the words are formed. Between sentence and proposition or statement no distinction is to be made.

Fortunately, though, Mallarmé and Valéry insisted that poetry is not constituted by ideas, expressed purely or otherwise. Poetry is made up of images and sounds.

> I bring you the child of an Idumaean night!
> Black, with wing bleeding, pale and unfeathered,
> Through the glass burnt with incense and gold,
> Through the panes, frozen, and still gloomy, alas
> The dawn burst forth in the lamp angelic,
> Palms! and when it had shown this relic
> To its father attempting an enemy smile,
> The blue and sterile solitude shuddered.
> O nursing mother, with your child and the innocence
> Of your cold feet, receive the horrible birth
> And with your voice recalling viol and clavacin,
> With your faded finger, will you press the breast
> Whence flows in sibylline whiteness woman
> For lips made hungry by the blue virgin air?[10]

The pure poet's attitude toward creativity and the poem created is therefore (1) that the poet in performing rites of beauty must radically dissociate language from its ordinary contextual functions so that it may attain its maximum suggestive and musical power; (2) that to do this one must separate oneself from the ordinary stuff of experience and find aesthetic (and metaphysical) meaning in the formal dimensions of one's art alone; and (3) that the poem created must be structured by a consistent feeling so that the poem may subsist in its own being as an articulated form.

* * *

"You have surely noticed," writes Valéry, "the curious fact that a certain *word*, which is perfectly clear when you hear or use it in *everyday* speech, and which presents no difficulty when caught up in the rapidity of an ordinary sentence, becomes mysteriously cumbersome, offers a strange resistance, defeats all efforts at definition, the moment you withdraw it from circulation for separate study and try to find its meaning after taking away its temporary function."[11] And little wonder! Language is not constituted of discrete sounds that can meaningfully stand in isolation from one another or from human action. Language, we have come to understand, is experienced in gestalt not in atomic terms; a word has meaning only in a communicative context with other words, uttered or implied, and as the linguistic complex is bound up with human experience. Although all linguistic communication has a personal dimension, Isabel Hungerland is no doubt correct when pointing out that "the associations that give connotation to a word must be communal, the result of shared experience."[12] When words become only pleasing sounds or rhythmic units, their nature as carriers of meaning is negated. And the mind that would originate them in this manner has negated itself as a giver of meaning.

There is something curious and, one suspects, something fundamentally wrong in any attempt to take one human power or capacity and raise it to a position of isolated pre-eminence. Any such attempt does violence to that very fundamental psychological fact of the interdependence between the emotional, intellectual, and spiritual aspects of human nature. One cannot think without feeling; and strength of thought, of insight, of intellect, rather than being opposed to strength of feeling is part of the feeling that has a significant place in art. Perhaps, because of this sundering of native intellectual power from a refined or aesthetised emotion, there is not infrequently a precious quality in the pure poem, a certain artificiality of feeling tone and rhythm. Surface form gets confounded with inner structure, with the order and articulation of elements that the experiencer rejoices in recognizing and contemplating.[13]

The pure poet condemns himself to perhaps the most difficult kind of isolation. By sanctifying the word, through withdrawing it from life into an atmosphere of holiness, he detaches himself from, but makes no effort to transcend, relational experience. He wants to retain his "intelligence," but by seeking to have it only in a purified, infallible form, he loses it: "The purer the glass the less we see it."

* * *

Mallarmé and Valéry have nevertheless (perhaps because they failed in their program) written some magnificent verse, and they have articulated one very important truth about poetry, namely that it is neither simply emotive discourse nor is it made-up of ideas which can be separated from their mode or style of expression; poetry is rather a genuine creation of experience. Although by its nature a poem is always a "sharing," it engenders experience rather than expresses it as such. Mallarmé and Valéry did discover the essence of poetry, *but they then confounded the essence with the poem itself; they attempted to make of the essence the thing.*

Poetry does involve a special rhythmic, imagistic, sensualistic (in the strict sense of the word) play of language formed by aesthetic demands of inner structure; the poem itself though, the poem taken as a complete entity that is experienced or is experienceable aesthetically, is a creation of, an embodiment, and a communicator of meaning. Referential and "pure" language elements combine inseparably in a poem. The poem itself is never merely musical, for its medium is language. Words are bound to human experience. A so-called nonsense verse must at least have this much sense if it is to function aesthetically; the experiencer must recognize that the implied referent of the poem is the world of ordinary speech and that the poet is indicating something with reference to that world (its mendacity, foolishness, or whatever) by means of his nonsense. "Pure nonsense" can never be experienced aesthetically; in fact it cannot be experienced at all. The utterly nonsensical can never pass beyond being a primitive sense datum. To be creative of experience a poem must, in short, relate to, and disclose something about, our ordinary life-experience with all its social and moral complexities while at the same time opening up new possibilities for that experience and thereby enriching it and ourselves.

8

Where Is a Dance?

> O body set to music, O
> brightening glance,
> How can we know the
> dancer from the dance?
> (Yeats)

Susanne K. Langer states that

> Dance is, in fact, the most serious intellectual business of savage life: it is the envisagement of a world beyond the spot and the movement of one's animal existence, the first conception of life as a whole—continuous, superpersonal life, punctuated by birth and death, surrounded and fed by the rest of nature. From this point of view, the prehistoric evolution of dancing does not appear strange at all. It is the very process of religious thinking, which begets the conceptions of "Powers" as it symbolizes them. To the "mythic consciousness" these creations are realities, not symbols; they are not felt to be created by the dance at all, but to be invoked, adjured, challenged or placated, as the case may be. The symbol of the world, the balletic realm of forces, *is* the world, and dancing is the human spirit's participation in it.[1]

Śiva dances—and thereby sustains the universe. The dancing god—the archetypal manifestation of spiritual energy. In "primitive" consciousness and in many traditional societies, as is often observed, a *ritual* performance is conceived not so much as a unique event but as a repetitive re-enactment. Rituals are performed, as it were, according to "scripts"—written or not. It is precisely the ability to perform a ritual correctly that allows for its efficacy. And so with dance; insofar as it remains true to its ritual origins, its kinesthetic power is felt by the dancer and discerned by the participant-spectator to be grounded in a reality outside of itself and to "center" (in Eliade's sense) that very reality. Each performance then is understood as a re-enactment of a primal event—and in this "allographic" sense the individual dancer, with his or her own "manner of movement," is of little consequence compared to the universalizing power generated in and through the exactitude of the performance. What is sought in ritual-based dance is attaining an identity between self and holy power and not an expression of an individual style. In ritual-based dance, style is subsumed in what is taken to be a timeless necessity.

A dance then belongs to the world that it centers. *A dance is located in the world sustained by its performance.*

* * *

John J. Martin writes:

> The pervasive presence of space . . . is the dancer's native realm, in much the same sense that air is the bird's or water the fish's, and it makes imperious demands upon both the performer and the composer. For the latter there is first of all the question of the amount of space to be employed and its character. Some compositions involve the extensive traversing of ground up to the utilization of the whole area available, while others unfold without change of base, that is, with the dancer remaining virtually in one spot.
>
> . . .
>
> In the matter of direction of movement, the forward and backward, the sideward, the diagonal, the curvilinear path, the broken line of progress, the turn in place, the shift of direction, all have definite values of their own.[2]

And the movements of dance also give rise to a space that is intrinsic to the dance and, as with time in the visual arts, has its own formal and expressive quality.

There is the "public space" of the actual environment *in* which the dance takes place and is shaped, in many ways, by its requirements; and there is the space that the dance itself defines and is to be found nowhere else than in the dance. This space is at once formal—created by the movements of the dancer and the design of the group composition, when it is not a solo dance[3]—and affective laden, as it gets surcharged, as it were, with aesthetic force. The space intrinsic to a dance becomes then a field of meaningful vitality; its meaningfulness derives from its rightness; its rightness having to do with the appropriateness of its *spacing*.

The space created by a dance is an aesthetic space constituted by dynamic relations that, when the space is aesthetically good, are discerned to have just that fitness which we recognize to constitute form. Quantitative, measurable space gives way to qualitative spacing—the result of what Maxine Sheets-Johnstone calls *thinking in movement*.

Whether a dance is narrative or abstract, expressive or imitative, by its nature as dance it creates spatial relations that themselves give rise to the conditions it consequently realizes. In short, a dance defines its own environment as much as it takes place in a measurable spatiality.

* * *

Where, then, is a dance? *A dance is where it is performed, the "where" being created by the dance.*

9

Form in Architecture

Form is present in a building when a "right relationship" obtains between the building's "structure" and its "shape."

Structure is the mode and manner of a building's construction; it is the embodied engineering, as it were, that the building utilizes and, insofar as it shows itself, exhibits.

Shape is the material mass and volume of the building in its environmental context; its spatial relations—interior and exterior.

All buildings thus have a structure and a shape, but not all buildings have a form. For instance, when the demand that a building have a specific shape (e.g., because of programmatic requirements that call for its yielding a certain economic return) with this demand in turn determining, to a considerable extent, the building's structure and shape (usually according to a building or zoning code)—your typical undistinguished office building in cities throughout the world—form is not likely to be present. *When structure and shape are so in accord with each other that the relation between them appears to be necessary, if not inevitable, form is present.*[1]

Now it might be objected that this notion of form is primarily a "modernist" one (congenial, say, to a Mies van der Rohe, with his dictum that "less is more") and fails thereby to encompass architectural works in traditional styles and in so-called postmodernism.[2] On the contrary, *form* as here defined does not commit one to any belief that, apart from taste, form must be pure, hence structure *ohne Ornament*. For the modernist, in what was once known as the international style, the absence of the superfluous shows a certain self-sufficiency, a spiritual integrity or wholeness that requires nothing outside of itself. Standing out from the social and the historical, eliminating all that is indeterminate and contingent, the modernist building is not, a postmodernist would assert, at home, as it were, in the here and now of this world; and it is, accordingly, boring.[3]

In any event, defining form as a relation between a building's structure and its shape does not in itself specify any particular architectural program.

The definition implies only that the aesthetic experience of a building as a work of architectural art consists essentially in the apprehension of a building's form. If one is unable to apprehend the form of a building (either because of one's own inadequacies or because the building in fact lacks form) one is unable to experience it as a successful work of architectural art.

One might further object, however, that this formalistic criteria does not, and cannot, do justice to the many other dimensions of one's experience of a building—the appreciation of its symbolic values, its social functions, or its historical style. But this objection can be answered by pointing out that these factors are extremely important for appreciating and understanding the building in its full cultural context and that they may contribute importantly to the richness of our experience, but that these factors are no substitute for the apprehension of the essential aesthetic quality of the building. One can indeed marvel at certain great monuments of the past (and those of the present that have unusual historical and social significance). One can understand them in terms of history, politics, religion, or economics, in terms of technological and stylistic development, and so on—and all of these factors may be important, I need repeat, in our experiencing the artwork, the building, in its own complete aesthetic being—but unless one apprehends the building's form (assuming it is there to be apprehended) one is not so much experiencing the building aesthetically as one is experiencing one's knowledge of it. In our experience of architecture especially we often confound a recognition of (historical) style with aesthetic experience proper. Many observers rest content with the appreciation of a building as soon as they notice that it is "Gothic" or "Romanesque" or "Neo-classical," and rejoice (as the case may be) in the merits of the style. But it is readily apparent that structures and shapes produce styles in architecture and not forms. To experience a building aesthetically as the aesthetic object that it is, one has to get behind the (historical) style, so to speak, and to the form. Any human artifact, in short, can be analyzed and understood in terms of a multiplicity of historical, social, economic perspectives, but something more is always needed if the object is to be experienced as a work of art. The incorporation of these perspectives into one's vision of the building might, once again, be a necessary condition for an enriched or fully developed experience; while the apprehension of form is assuredly a sufficient condition for the *essential* aesthetic experience of a building.

But this does not, of course, mean that all apprehensions of form are of equal aesthetic value. Some forms elicit but little interest or attention; others, perhaps because of the complexity of the elements that enter into their relationship, demand an in-depth engagement; and some others "radiate." This is certainly the case, as we have seen, with every type of artwork, and as with other types, one cannot specify what conditions make a form radiate. The factors one might be tempted to articulate or enumerate, such as "correct proportion" or "proper harmonization" usually turn out to be aesthetically meaningless without appealing to the very notion of radiance or beauty that one is seeking to define. And more important, we realize today that what makes a form radiate or be beautiful is within the province of the unique creative power of the artist and the informed sensitivity of the participant of the work. No analysis of the creative process yields a formula for rightness of any interesting scope or validity, and no analysis of the constituents of the object discloses how they are "put together" to make a qualitative whole. One can tell if form is present, one can perhaps know why it is absent; but one cannot explain why a particular form radiates.

* * *

The preceding analysis of form perhaps makes clear why buildings are so seldom experienced by us as works of art, and why aestheticians find it so difficult to speak meaningfully about architecture. To apprehend the form of a building, let alone a radiant form, demands that one know a considerable amount about shape and structure.

Architecture is rather singular among the arts in its strict dependence upon "actualities." A building is an occasion for the play of external elements upon it (light, the weather) and these externalities affect the shape of a building more than in any other kind of artwork. A building must confront external elements (incorporate them, adjust to them)—for there is no other place to which it can go—as much as it must mold the materials that constitute it as such.

The relationship of a building to its site is likewise an integral aspect of its shape. No matter what attitude the architect takes to his or her site, the site becomes a crucial factor in the shape that is created. The site may be "rejected" in terms of any attempt to integrate organically the building with it (as in Wright's Guggenheim Museum in New York City),[4] the building may be happily integrated with the site (as in Fallingwater), or the building may be utterly subordinated to the site (staying with Wright, as in his Wisconsin home built *into* a hill)—in all cases the relation of the site to the building becomes an inescapable feature of the building's shape.[5]

To experience the shape of a building one must physically enter the building and mentally participate in its complex spatial relationships. One must move through the interior space; and while thus preoccupied with only a part of the building's space, one must struggle to see the building constantly as a whole. One must grasp the virtual as well as real space of the building. One can do this quite readily with a painting or a piece of sculpture, for these make themselves more or less available immediately as wholes; one can do this only with great effort with a building.

Although in a sense a building may be said to define the laws to which it is subject, it nevertheless remains subject to physical conditions (e.g., gravity) to a far greater extent than do the other arts, and this makes it extremely difficult for one to grasp its structure. One must know something about what is actually occurring with the structural members; one must know something about the strength of the materials used, the demands placed on them, the distribution of forces throughout them. Only a few observers will detect that a structure, say, is overbuilt. And in many cases the structure is purposely hidden underneath an elaborate ornamentation—or, as with much recent postmodernist work, disguised within a complex juxtaposition of seemingly "contradictory" (to use Robert Venturi's expression) elements taken from diverse historical styles—so that it is impossible for anyone but a highly trained observer to know what is occurring in the structure. If architecture is "frozen music," then most persons are more aware of the "frozenness" than of the music.

But the demand for a knowledge of structure cannot be too stringent, for then only a structural engineer (and only some architects) would be capable of apprehending a building's form, and this is surely not the case. It is possible for a sensitive observer to realize the direction of forces and sympathetically feel the tensions, the stresses and strains at work in the structure. A structure is something more than mere "statics"; it is rather a vital system, a creation of dynamic forces—and one can, to a considerable extent, get at this intuitively.

In sum, the essential aesthetic perception of an architectural work of art, I believe, centers on the apprehension of its form, which may be defined as a right relationship obtaining between the building's structure and its shape. We seldom perceive buildings aesthetically because of our everyday, practical relations with them and because of the special difficulties involved in the apprehension of their forms. But these difficulties are not insurmountable, and when surmounted, one is able to apprehend a building precisely as a work of art.

10

Music as Silence-and-Sound

Music is sound. Noise is sound. The difference between music and noise is silence. Let me explain.

Ontologically, there is a silence that is pure being, without beginning or end. A plenitude, this silence constitutes, as it were, the prebeginning of sound. When one is attuned to this silence, this "essential" depth of being, any sound, any utterance or expression appears only as a subtraction from what already is. And yet a prolonged dwelling in this original silence extinguishes the person as well as all sound and thus in its completeness becomes unendurable, and so music, which is grounded in this silence and enables us to have a very special relation to it. Yet music goes even further, as it is a creative articulation of silence from among its infinite possibilities to be heard in our experience: Music is *articulated* silence-and-sound. And yet this hearing requires a listening that brings the hearer, when the music is profound, safely back to the beginingless fullness of being that is the primal silence. The highest musical art is thus not a triumph over silence (or a Wagnerian replacement of it) but an active participation in its primitive power.

Many dimensions of silence, then, are present in and as music. First of all is the primal or original silence, which is the ground of sound and becomes for music a surrounding silence that is ever present within the work, functioning as it does as its "context." Every musical composition incorporates a surrounding silence into itself—happily or unhappily, depending on whether it works in harmony with or in alienation from it. Music always has a *nearness* to silence, an ever-presentness that is its dwelling place.

This may perhaps be clarified by saying that *communication*, if it means anything at all, is something that certainly takes place in music; and just assuredly a silence is present that is one of the conditions for its occurrence. This silence contains what is unsounded but is soundable, just as in speech we always have what is unsaid but is sayable (along with what is said). This silence is a reservoir of sound possibilities. It itself is not articulated: In itself it has neither a formal nor expressive function or presence. It is present only as the context of possibilities relevant for the particular musical work. In a musical work that is right for itself, this silence is never experienced as a mere absence of sound but as that which is surcharged with potential musical value.

Music, we have said, is an "articulation" of silence-and-sound. Music differs from noise precisely in taking up silence as constitutive of its very being and, formally, syntactically, as it were, having that silence become integral to its dynamic sound structure; and, expressively, semantically, as it were, allowing that silence to function dramatically, contributing to the affective tonality (the joy, the sadness) that might be present. Noise, in short, is a kind of violation of silence; music is its very formulation.

Eduard Hanslick called music "moving figures of sound." And Leonard B. Meyer has pointed out that "Understanding music is not merely a matter of perceiving separate sounds. It involves relating sounds to one another in such a way that they form patterns (musical events). Furthermore, smaller patterns combine with one another to form larger, more extensive ones—patterns in high architectonic levels. These in turn influence the further development of patterns on both lower and higher levels. Thus the implications of patterns on the several architectonic levels exist simultaneously and interact with one another."[1]

But the condition for perceiving "separate sounds" and the forming of them into patterns, musical events, which then become hierarchically organized, is the silence that allows for sound differentiation, the distinguishing of individual phrases and the like, and is a silence that is not only that in which sound dissolves and disappears but is itself heard as part of the musical work. The Gregorian chant, no less than the Bach fugue, knows the meaning of music as silence-and-sound. As indeed do non-Western musical traditions like the classical Indian, with its extemporaneous patterns brought forth within a predetermined rhythmical structure, the *tāla*; its setting forth of an initial beat, the *sama*, to which the performers return simultaneously, providing a silence of temporary closure; and a musical duration or interval, the *laya*, which informs throughout, both formally and expressively, the *jāti*, or ascending and descending scales that structure the typical composition or *rāga*. Other examples would be the Balinese *gamelan*, with its blending of background silence and sound, silence here not so much articulated in the intervals and pauses but rather by means of the continuous bell-like sounds of the tuned gongs and flutes, formulated as a pervading quality, and much of Japanese theater music, with its piercing sharp sounds produced by the striking of sticks and drums and shrieklike vocalizations, accentuating the silence that becomes the other side of the highly differentiated sounds. In short, silence is always formally constitutive of music. Let us contrast this with natural rhythmic sound patterns.

Waterfalls, ocean waves incessantly pounding on shore, and the like differ from music not only in terms of their relatively simple regularity but precisely in their not intending or achieving a creative articulation and presenceing of silence. There is, of course, the silence that, as absence of sound, allows the rhythmic pattern to be heard, but it is not a silence perceived as a basis of sound significance nor as that articulated with purposive aesthetic meaning. With a natural rhythmic sound pattern, silence is simply *given* with it; with music, silence is *created* and becomes formally constitutive of it.

The silence that determines and is determined in a musical rhythm, a melody, is thus experienced always as a kind of freedom, a spontaneity that comes with discipline and skill. Unlike with natural sound patterns, we recognize in music the ongoing possibilities that it itself gives rise to and their actualization in terms of the expressive values inherent in the work.

Just as in various life situations where, by not saying something, everything gets expressed (approval or disapproval; horror and shock, or surprise and delight; incomprehension or a comprehension that requires no further affirmation), so in music the expressive range of the unsaid, the unstated, the unannounced, is limitless yet acquires a specificity, a particular affective character, that is readily recognized and heard. Aristotle tells us that music is the most "imitative" of the arts. "Rhythm and melody supply imitations of anger and gentleness, and also of courage and temperance, and of all the qualities contrary to these, and of the other qualities of character . . . as we know from our own experience, for in listening to such strains our souls undergo a change."[2]

Silence, expressively, semantically, is, when successfully articulated, a *dramatic* silence. In the work of a master composer like Haydn, the silences are more than formal rests, they are full of expectations, of tensions; together with the sounds heard they define the affective qualities of the work. In music there are unexpected silences just as there are surprising sounds.

In musical works that fail to be right for themselves, the silence that is potentially dramatic is experienced as an absence, a negation. This "fallen" silence, if we may so call it, appears always as aesthetically meaningless in relation to the sound; it becomes only a place for listening to oneself, encouraging a self-indulgence that detaches interest and attention from the music in favor of our own wayward conscious meandering. Fallen silence is precisely the denial of the expressive musical possibilities of silence.

* * *

Music is essentially an art of performance and hence there are what we might call *performing silences*. There is the silence of the audience, both individually and collectively, that formally allows the work to proceed and, depending on the occasion, expressively is often filled with high expectations and anticipations of what is to be heard. There is also an audience silence that, in varying degrees, seems to participate directly in the performance as it is carried out, contributing to its vitality. And there is the silence that defines the performances' completion—not just formally when the work ends but when the audience leaves. It is the silence that gathers the final applause into itself and brings closure to the event.

Part III

11

Interpreting Art

Heidegger, Gadamer, and others in what may now be called the *hermeneutic tradition* would have us believe that *all* is interpretation; that understanding, interpreting, is foundational to our being in the world. Well perhaps so; but if so, it consists of very different kinds of activities and is carried out in many varied ways—with artwork interpretation being very much of its own kind and having its own distinctive way.

If it is the case that we always see meaningfully and affectively then interpretation is not something that is simply superadded to perception (Danto, "no knowledge of an object can make it look different; . . . an object retains its sensory qualities unchanged however it is classed and whatever way it may be called"[1]), rather it is integral to one's immediate as well as mediate experience. And with artwork experience, we have one of the richest possible integrations, for we come to the artwork with the awareness that an interpretative task is central to our experience of it; we *anticipate* the need to have a mode of attention that is throughout interpretive in character.

Artwork interpretation, as distinct from an immediate apprehension of what something is (e.g., identifying a familiar physical object as being of a certain kind) or grasp of what an everyday utterance might mean, always involves ambiguities. If I am told "Please shut the door" in a context where it is evident that this is a request (and not say a secret coded message) I need not "interpret" the utterance beyond my obtaining an understanding of what is intended by it. "*Who, if I cried, would hear me among the angelic/orders?*"[2] on the other hand, points toward a meaning and is a meaning "evident" only on the exercise of a reader's own imagination and intelligence as he or she stands in relation to the line and the poem of which it is a part and acknowledges its multivalent character. Poetic meaning is both *intended* and *intimated*—and their union in the word, the image, the sound gives rise to the possibilities that call for interpretation.

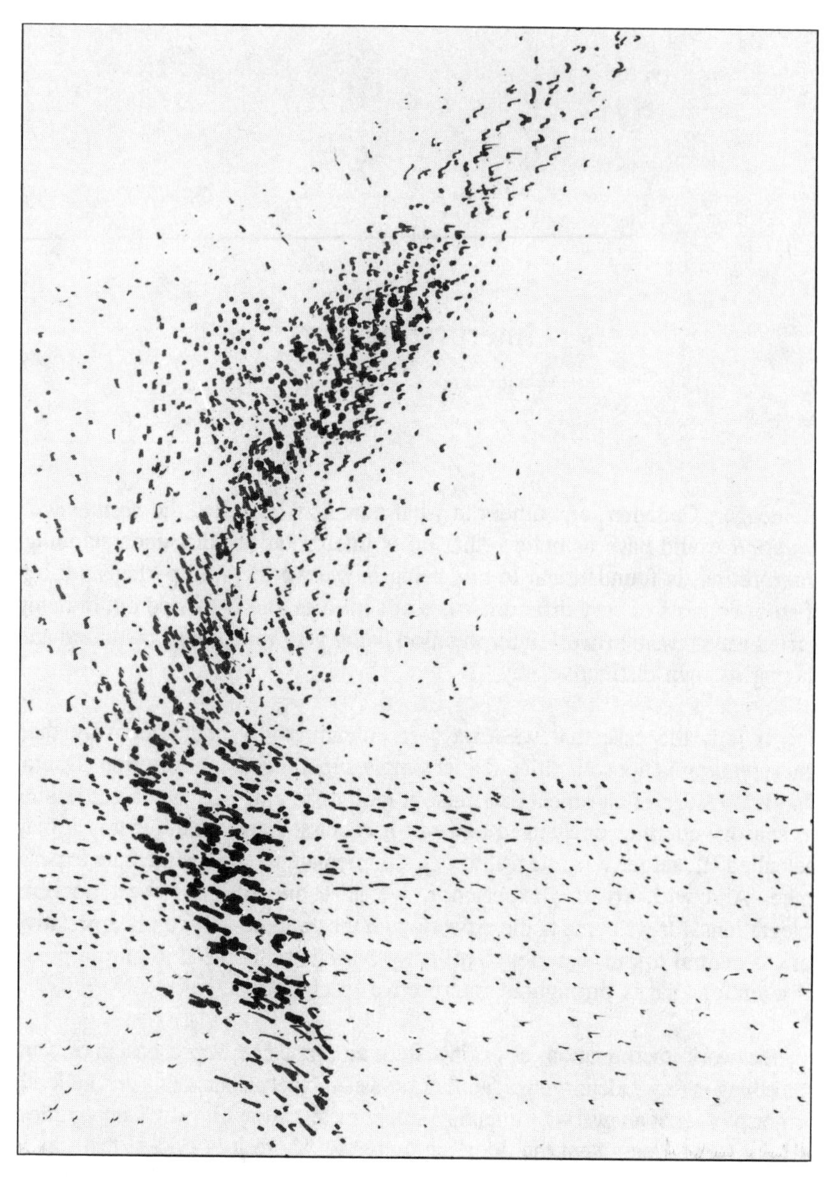

Figure 11.1. Nicolas de Stael. *Birds in Flight*, 1951. Felt-tip pen on paper. 71.7 x 51.4 cm. The Phillips Collection, Washington D.C.

Nicolas de Stael's Birds in Flight *shows what it means for a "many" (a group) and not a "one" (a particular thing) to be "in flight." The felt-tip pen markings represent birds without any marking being singularly identified as such; the markings show the "in flight" of the birds directly through the dynamic patterning, through the delicate shadings that give direction to the eye, through the tension created between the soaring, sweeping mass and the more stable, yet potentially rising, elements from below.*

Interpreting art is therefore not a matter of disambiguating an image, symbol, metaphor so that it may be rendered "literal" in another discourse but of preserving its meaning as an intention and intimation so that it may show itself as precisely the content that it is.

The title given to a work by the artist will often serve to organize interpretive perception in certain ways, signaling as it does an overall intention that the work strives to embody. Klee's *Heavenly and Earthly Time* might indeed be seen by a perceptive observer as being "about" temporality without the viewer having read the title; but most observers need to be guided by the title to see the criss-crossing lines as temporal interactions anchored in concentrated point instants as the thematic meaning of the work.

We interpret familiar things, we have suggested, in a rather immediate, unself-conscious, habituated way—recognizing them for the kinds of things they are, and so on. Our interpretation as to what the familiar thing is and what particular qualities as well it might possess, is self-validating; which is to say, we assume our "reading" is correct until such time as it proves otherwise.

We interpret alien things, on the other hand, in a different manner. We struggle first of all to bring the thing into some familiar region of our experience; to transform, in short, its alien character into something more congenial to our understanding. Interpretation here requires a continual negotiation, as it were, between our understanding and the thing and frequently involves just that hermeneutical circle of our moving from part to whole and whole back to part that is carried out so frequently in our engagements with texts. We domesticate the alien while at the same time seeking to expand and alter our own range and depth of understanding in virtue of our encounter with it. And we are never assured or take for granted that our initial interpretation is correct or that it is whole and complete.

Artwork interpretation is essentially akin to the interpretation of the alien.

Artwork interpretation ought properly to be directed toward the work as a whole; which is to say, to its aesthetic content and not to its subject matter alone. But then the question quite naturally arises: What is being interpreted and how does interpretation differ from some kind or other of informed recognition?

The answer would seem to be that anything in the work, including its expressive values, which calls for connectedness to everything else in the work—and to our life experience—is the proper "object" of interpretation and that interpretation, then, at its very best, precisely does not differ from informed recognition but is rather identical to it. Recognition is a mode of understanding, of "seeing"; it is an *insight into* the formed content of the work.

> The ideal of complete and undivided consciousness, where will and capability, thought and action, vision and realisation are one, is the highest Man can form, and yet, so impossible is it for Man to realise this ideal, to become like the Angels, that it is rather a rebuke than an inspiration. . . . And yet, declares Rilke, the highest kind of love is that which is unrequited, which is content simply to endure and, thereby, to *become*. Let us, then, since the Angels are too immeasurably beyond us, take as our examples the great lovers, and, also, those who have died young, through reflexion on whose destiny we shall achieve an intuition, which will still more deeply reconcile us to the fact of our transitoriness, into the unity of life and death and the complementariness of sorrow and joy.[3]

If the meaning of an artwork is its aesthetic content, and not some kind of relation between the work and something outside of it, then necessarily that meaning is irreducible. In varying degrees, however, depending on the particular work and its genre, a work's meaning need always be stated in a discourse different from that of the work. Statements about what an artwork means will thus never be purely descriptive but will always be partly interpretive.

Interpretation is a kind of translation from one domain of meaning to another; and, therefore, as with all translation, it does not make sense to hold to the possibility of a single, correct rendering or articulation. Artwork interpretation can never be guided by the two-valued language of "true" or "false," but only by degrees of "adequate" or "inadequate," "better" or "worse," "rich" or "impoverished"; the ideal interpretation occurring when the *reading into* coincides with the widest range of what is *readable out of* the work.[4]

Umberto Eco writes:

> Medieval interpreters were wrong in taking the world as a univocal text; modern interpreters are wrong in taking every text as an unshaped world. Texts are the human way to reduce the world to a manageable format, open to an intersubjective interpretive discourse. Which means that, when symbols are inserted into a text, there is, perhaps, no way to decide which interpretation is the "good" one, but it is still possible to decide, on the basis of the context, which one is due, not to an effort of understanding "that" text, but rather to a hallucinatory response on the part of the addressee.[5]

Normally we have greater confidence in our judgment that someone's interpretation is a "bad" one than that it is a "good" one, for the "bad" clearly shows itself as inadequate in a variety of possible ways; for example, (1) it does not conform to any reading of the language presented that is common to a given community of language users (if in recent times in English a poet were to say "A rose is a rose is a rose" and an interpreter insisted that the author was talking about or that the text as such refers to rocks, we could be quite assured that the interpreter was mistaken, if not deranged), (2) it does not carry one semantically any further than the most literal conceptual reading (the interpreter allows that "A rose is a rose . . ." is just stating a tautology, (3) if it calls for associations of meanings that the text in its own historical context could not have reasonably entertained (that *rose* is intended to symbolize "the finitude of human existence"), and so on.

Let us return to a portrait—a portrait as an interpretation (and not now as that which is itself to be interpreted). As an interpretation, a portrait strives to present an understanding of its object, the particular person being portrayed; an understanding that knows itself to be necessarily partial and incomplete yet hopefully insightful.

A portrait does not aspire to be an accurate copy, a low-level "imitation" of the person portrayed, for such an aspiration were it realized would precisely negate what it means to interpret something. An accurate copy, if it were possible to have one, tells us nothing more that what our own seeing of the object would reveal. A portrait must re-present the object, it must be a *reading* of the person portrayed.

And this further shows nicely how interpretation can be better or worse without there being, even in principle, a one, right reading. If one were to define the latter as that which disclosed all that can be presently known of the object, it would still be incomplete; there would always remain the surprising, the disclosing of something new, in future experience.[6] Artwork interpretation is not a matter of strict prediction but of subtle anticipation.

Artworks that are true are nevertheless authoritative in that they possess a compeling power to draw us to them and to control the determination of their meaning. This does not mean that an artwork that is true imposes a single correct interpretation on us; rather it means that the artwork always retains its primacy in setting what is appropriate (and indeed permissible) for its understanding.

Gadamer, following Heidegger, has argued quite convincingly that interpretation always starts from an interpreter's own "fore projections" or "prejudices," which give rise to certain expectations or anticipations of meaning, which preconceptions themselves get altered in the course of one's engagement with the work. "Interpretation begins with pre-conceptions that are replaced by more suitable ones."[7] In short, our expectations of meaning must always yield to the authority of the work.

The title "Birds in Flight" directs us to see the marks as birds, rather than, say, as bees.

Kant grounded the judgment of taste, of beauty in pleasure, but is not such "pleasure" associated with the apprehension of aesthetic content, of meaningful form? Is it not of a fundamentally different kind from that of other sense-based pleasures, with the difference not resting, as Kant would have it, on its "disinterestedness" or its being liberated form all conceptuality, but on the requirement of concentration with its accompanying unself-consciousness? At times Kant comes close to this when he argues that the ground of a particular aesthetic pleasure lies in "the harmony of the faculties" (of imagination and understanding); but still he disallows the distinctive cognitive/affective mode of concentrated consciousness that is essential to artwork interpretation.

If all genuine understanding involves an appropriation, a making as one's own, of that which is sought to be understood (a "fusion of horizons" as hermeneutics rather dramatically, and sometimes obscurely, puts it), then artwork understanding in particular requires much more than just a noticing of various qualities. It requires an assimilation of the full intentionality of the work. Artwork interpretation becomes then a mode of enhanced self-understanding as well as an understanding of a work.

> True, it is strange to inhabit the earth no longer,
> to use no longer customs scarcely acquired,
> not to interpret roses, and other things
> that promise so much, in terms of a human future;
> to be no longer all that one used to be
> in endlessly anxious hands, and to lay aside
> even one's proper name like a broken toy.
> Strange, not to go on wishing one's wishes. Strange.
> to see all that was once relation so loosely fluttering
> hither and thither in space. And it's hard, being dead,
> and full of retrieving before one begins to espy
> a trace of eternity.—Yes, but all of the living
> make the mistake of drawing too sharp distinctions.
> Angels, (they say) are often unable to tell
> whether they move among living or dead. The eternal
> torrent whirls all the ages through either realm
> for ever, and sounds above their voices in both.[8]

In the "Elegies," Rilke wrote to his Polish translator, AFFIRMATION OF LIFE AND AFFIRMATION OF DEATH REVEAL THEMSELVES AS ONE. To concede the one without the other is, as is here experienced and celebrated, a restriction that finally excludes all infinity. Death is our reverted, our unilluminated, SIDE OF LIFE: we must try to achieve the greatest possible consciousness of our existence, which is at home in BOTH OF THESE UNLIMITED PROVINCES, which is INEXHAUSTIBLY NOURISHED OUT OF BOTH.[9]

If an artwork is a world, then it is clear that the author (the poet, the painter, the composer, . . .) has no authoritative position with regard to the possible richness of meaning his or her work might possess. The author, although in some ways privileged with regard to the work's meaning, stands nevertheless to the work with much the same wonderment as that of the viewer. The author assuredly points the direction, sets the parameters, one might say, to the work's meaning so that the work may guide its own interpretation, but others very likely will always find appropriate connections to their own experience that were neither anticipated nor recognized by the author.[10]

The old, but still lively, debate over a presumed "intentional fallacy," which would look to the degree to which an author's intention is realized in the work as a criterion for its success, needs, then, to take a more hermeneutical turn. Certainly, the artist's intention (aesthetically speaking and not motivationally) must be realized in the work if it is to be of any aesthetic interest, and we need not look elsewhere to find it if it is not so realized. Also, seldom, especially with modern art, has the artist a clearly defined intention in advance of the work's making, rather the intention comes forth and is developed throughout the process of the work's coming into being. Nevertheless, on the meaning as distinct for the moment from the evaluative side, what we may know both internally to the work and externally from other sources about the author's intention in pointing to various possibilities of meaning can be extremely relevant and important. This is especially the case with historical works. To experience say a Greek tragedy rightly we need to know a good deal about Greek life, its ideas, values, social organization, spiritual concerns—"rightly" having more of a negative (not getting it wrongly) than a positive import; which is to say, in agreement with Gadamer, that it is not a matter of retrieving some original meaning of the work that we can establish with assurance from historical sources, but in our own time, we are engaging the work not capriciously but in terms of what it itself is. In the last analysis it will always be the work that intends, but only in virtue of an author and participant-viewer, which of course brings us to "desconstruction."

Derrida writes:

> we shall designate by the term *differance* the movement by which language . . . becomes "historically" constituted as a fabric of differences.[11]

> Differance is what makes the movement of signification possible only if each element that is said to be "present," appearing on the stage of presence, is related to something other than itself but retains the mark of a past element and already lets itself be hallowed out by the mark of its relation to a future element.[12]

Differance, we are told, "is the fact that meaning can never be accounted for in terms of punctual self-presence; that language is not only (as Saussure argued) a *differentiated* structure of contrasts and relationships 'without positive terms', but also that meaning is endlessly *deferred* along the chain of linguistic substitutions and displacements that occur whenever we seek to define what a given term signifies in context."[13]

But surely meaning, linguistic or other, is not "endlessly deferred" except in cases of extraordinary ambiguity; rather we all the time make an accommodation with the text with which we are comfortable, satisfied that we are on the right track of understanding, and go about our business.

But it is Derrida's insistence that "there is simply no deciding just what is 'intrinsic' to the artwork and what belongs either *to* or *outside* the frame,"[14] which is, hermeneutically, entirely bewildering—for we continually make those determinations and with good reasons when we are called upon to offer them. Assuredly, in some issues involving interpretation, the inside/outside duality is blurred (and indeed ought to be dispensed with), but otherwise we see clearly enough *where* the artwork is and what are the boundaries within which we carry out our interpretive activities.

Nelson Goodman asks: "Does a work mean just whatever anyone says it means, or is there a difference between right and wrong statements about how and what it means?"[15] And he answers:

> On one view, correct interpretation is unique; there are no alternatives, and rightness is tested by accord with the artist's intentions. . . . But the main fault I find in this view lies in its absolutism. . . . A work of art typically means in varied and contrasting and shifting ways and is open to many equally good and enlightening interpretations.
>
> At the opposite extreme from such absolutism is a radical relativism that takes any interpretation to be as right or wrong as any other. Everything goes if anything does. . . . A work of art means whatever it may be said to mean—or, in other words, it doesn't mean at all.
>
> The resolute desconstructionist . . . will dismiss unconstrued works as will-o-the-wisps and treat interpretation not as *of* anything but as mere storytelling. . . .
>
> A third view that might be called constructive relativism takes deconstruction as a prelude to reconstruction and insists in recognition that among the construals of a work some—even some that conflict with one another—are right while others are wrong. Consideration of what constitutes the difference thus becomes obligatory.[16]

All interpretation involves evaluation, for a disclosure of meaning is always carried out in selecting/rejecting ways and is guided in the first place, as we have noted, by the prejudgments (the "prejudices") of the interpreter. Artwork interpretation in particular is thus never a mechanical sort of activity, one that could be done by a properly programmed computer, for although interpretation is a kind of translation, no mere matching of linguistic elements could ever take one very far. The artwork, Gadamer rightly reminds us, "speaks to us as a work and not as a bearer of a message."[17]

Artwork interpretation is thus dissimilar to dream interpretation. The interpretation of dreams presupposes that a causal explanatory account can be given that would allow for a "correct" interpretation of its symbols. This is analytically presupposed in the very idea that dream marks are "symbols," some "mechanism" (in Freud's sense) is at work that necessitates the particular symbol in the context of an individual's experience.[18] Artwork interpretation, on the other hand, does, to be sure, involve some grasp of the creative process by which the work has come into being, but not in causal explanatory terms as such, rather in those directly relevant to the process itself (the kinds of choices at play and so on) with the recognition that the work's meaning is fundamentally irreducible. Artwork meaning is not a disguised showing, a bearer of a hidden message, it is a vital presentation of itself—its interpretation requiring therefore aesthetic sensitivity and artwork understanding.

> Every Angel is terrible. Still, though, alas!
> I invoke you, almost deadly birds of the soul,
> knowing what you are.[19]

> In the *First Elegy* affirmation, on the whole, predominates over negation, and praise, or celebration, over lament. The limitations of Man have been recognized, but it has been suggested that they may, perhaps, be the conditions of a special kind of activity. Nevertheless, the value of an affirmation depends on the weight of conquered negation behind it, and in the succeeding *Elegies* it is negation that predominates, insistence on the limitations of Man.[20]

We interpret individual artworks in relation to other works within a given tradition as much as we do in relation to our *Lebenswelt*. Art interpretation is therefore always bound up with specific cultural contexts. Aesthetic meaning, in other words, as we have seen, is not determinable only with reference to the work's autonomy but requires as well some reference to the cultural or historical standards and expectations that inform the very manner of its coming into being. Hence the extraordinary difficulty one has in interpreting works from traditions very different from one's own.

Does Birds in Flight, *then, mean that nature exhibits a purposiveness—birds in flight always going somewhere, as in migration? Or does it mean that nature exhibits a free play of movement for its own sake—birds spontaneously grouping themselves in ever-shifting dynamic patterns?*

We familiarize our worlds in order to acquire a certain ease of consciousness, a retreat from an otherwise exhausting attentiveness. This enables us as well to expand our awareness from the specious present to larger, extended domains of experience. With the unfamiliar, the alien, there is an uneasiness, a disquietude, which confuses and binds us to it, until some degree of familiarity (or mere shutting-out) is achieved. The alien does, however, when responded to in a spirit of playful openness, compel a sense of the mystery of being: The familiar tempts us to take everything for granted.

How often has one, while visiting a large museum, rested satisfied with casually identifying various masterworks as being the work of so-and-so or as tokens of a historical type, as though that recognition constituted an adequate reading of the work. The alien work calls for an engagement quite other than that of authorial recognition or the placing it in a "school" or broad historical period. And something is rightfully alien about all great works of art.

Does Birds in Flight, *with its suggestiveness, economy of expression, and apparent spontaneity belong as much to an East Asian art tradition as it does to the contemporary West?*

With artworks, do we interpret only what is said, stated, presented or do we also appropriate its horizon of the unsaid, the unstated, the unpresented—and the unsayable—that accompanies it?

Heidegger (and in many ways Sartre after him) insisted that our encounter with things always involves a standing-out of the object against a background of what is not announced within the context of our attention and interest and that this "absence" is a constitutive part of what is meant in consciousness as an event of our understanding. What this comes down to for art interpretation is that our assimilation of what is presented brings with it something of both the immediate perceptual context of the experience and the historical placement of the work as it is within the compass of our present experience and as it has its own being within the historicity that informs it without being present as such within it. The unsaid *belongs* with the said and points in the direction of the unsayable, the silence from which the work derived and to which it returns.

In "Against Interpretation," written in 1964, prior to the widespread popularity of philosophical hermeneutics, Susan Sontag argued that interpretation, which she understood to be the reduction of a work to its content and thus to what the content supposedly meant when translated into a discursive "aboutness," was not only superfluous (a genuine work simply shows what it means) but pernicious (an assault upon the work, a triumph of mediocrity, a replacement of the formal achievement of art with mundane, often portentous, and usually pretentious meanings).[21]

Arthur Danto now argues what appears to be the antithesis of this position, stating as he does that it his view "that whatever appreciation may come to, it must in some sense be a function of interpretation. . . . Interpretation consists in determining the relationship between a work of art and its material counterpart."[22]

But interpretation, we argue, when proper, is directed toward the aesthetic content of the work; toward, that is to say, the full intentionality of the work to be aesthetically forceful, meaningful, and beautiful. Interpretation, when carried out properly, thus always preserves and seeks to enhance the integrity of the work.

Figure 11.2. School of Geiami. *Jittoku Laughing at the Moon*, Late 15th Century. Ink on paper. 77.7 x 40 cm. Fenollosa-Weld Collection. Courtesy, Museum of Fine Arts, Boston

Even in everyday language use, in conversation, interpretation is not directed toward subject matter alone, but toward the "style" as well of what is said. Who says what and how is integral to the meaning of what is said. Artwork meaning, and therefore its interpretation, is an intensification of this quite ordinary communicative situation. And it is something much more—for it involves as well something of the *absurd*.

* * *

The absurd liberates.

Absurdity is the rejection of the expectation of meaning. It is the affirmation of the utter indifference of being and the recognition that this indifference is as it should be. Laughing, screaming, weeping mean nothing at all—and only then do they mean everything.

Absurdity is the consciousness of the infinite possibility of no meaning. It is the recognition of the pretense in all meaning-laden schemes; it is the understanding that the suffering is only theirs for whom the self is already lost.

The monk laughs *with* the moon. Neither cares—for they are where they belong.

The absurd liberates. But there is no *way* to it that would not be either comic or tragic and therefore the wrong way.

* * *

In art the "amateur" artist or critic rather than the master artist or connoisseur confounds the whimsical with the absurd. The whimsical operates at the same level as the meaning laden, bordering as it does on the meaningless. No-meaning, the absurd, occupies its own place, different in kind from the meaningful and the meaningless. The absurd is never trivial.

The experiencer of an artwork must, in the end, become a participant in the absurdity that the artwork opens up, the space of radical discontinuity, of play, of the unique vitality that is the work. Interpretation must yield to the consciousness of no-meaning.

The absurd in art, then, is not just play, it is a surplus, an abundance of play, with the artist outplaying, as it were, the very conditions of creativity.

Art, by its very nature, is a celebration of the absurd as well as its being a world of meaning.

12

Truth in Art

One of the supreme ironies of Western intellectual history is that Plato (that consummate philosophical poet) first introduced serious confusions about the relationship between truth and art, confusions that center first of all on his applying a simple correspondence criterion of truth, which is drawn from truth of statements (or beliefs) to art. Plato (*Republic*, Bk. 10), as we have seen, finds the artist lacking powers of knowable insight and thus reduced to making copies of objects that are themselves only poor refections of their rational forms or Ideas, with the copies never accurately depicting the sensible objects due to the necessary perspectival character of any attempt to do so. The poet (of the *Ion* and *Phaedrus*) is a kind of mad demiurgos, mindlessly (without the employ of reason) making his world. For Plato, although certain kinds of works of art may have educative value (see his *Laws*), there is no truth in art; for the artist simply does not know whereof he speaks.[1]

Aristotle agreed with Plato that truth is essentially a matter of correspondence, but he found this truth to be somewhat irrelevant for art. According to Aristotle, "Any impossibilities there may be in his [a poet's] descriptions of things are faults. But from another point of view they are justifiable, if they serve the end of poetry itself . . . [e.g.,] it is a lesser error in an artist not to know . . . that the hind has no horns, than to produce an unrecognizable picture of one."[2]

In aesthetics, following Plato and Aristotle, the problem of truth in art has been formulated primarily in the context of accepting the primacy of propositional truth, and within that framework it has been repeatedly asked whether there is truth (of a propositional kind) in art and what, if any, is its aesthetic relevance.[3]

But propositional truth or statement truth is only one among many several uses and senses of *truth*. As I have pointed out elsewhere,

> In the Latin *veritas*, the Sanskrit *satya*, the Arabic *haqq*, "truth" and "reality" are closely identified. Truth is not just a property of statements, propositions

> or beliefs; it is a quality of being, of human beings and human activities. In the English language, on the other hand, the word "truth" (or "true") is used quite explicitly in at least three basic ways: (1) as the manner in which things are in themselves or the manner in which the world is in itself; truth as reality, truth as being—*truth as opposed to nonbeing or the purely fictional*; (2) as genuineness of a thing—'Yeats is a true poet'; 'These are true pearls'; truth as the conformity of a thing to our idea, definition, or conception of the thing—*truth as opposed to the counterfeit, the fake*; and (3) as a property of a statement, proposition or belief, usually as the linguistic or mental entity is thought to correspond to or with what is in fact the case—*truth as opposed to the erroneous, the false*.[4]

Heidegger, perhaps more than any other modern philosopher, tried to formulate a conception of truth that does not assume the primacy of propositional truth as such and to integrate that conception into an understanding of art.[5] Tracing the concept of truth back to its early Greek origins as *alethia*, "unconcealedness," Heidegger argues that truth is a discovery, a "showing forth" of an object or what he calls an *essent*. In language somewhat less dense than Heidegger's, J. L. Mehta explicates the teaching in this way: "What perception establishes is nothing other than *that* it actually *is* the essent itself which was meant in the statement, that the statement-making relation to what is stated is a shining forth of the essent, that it *discovers* the essent about which it is. What is evidenced is the discovering character of the statement. The essent meant in the judgment shows itself so as it is in itself; it is in itself so as the statement shows forth or discovers it to be."[6] Truth, Heidegger is then able to say "does not possess its original seat in the proposition."[7]

> All behaviour is "overt" (lit. "stands open": *offenständig*) to what-is, and all "overt" relationship is behaviour. Man's "overtness" varies with the nature of what-is and the mode of behaviour. All working and carrying out of tasks, all transaction and calculation, sustains itself in the open, an overt region within which what-is can expressly take up its stand *at* and *how* it is *what* it is, and thus become capable of expression. This can only occur when what-is represents itself (*selbst vorstelling wird*) with the representative statement, so that the statement submits to a directive enjoining it to express what-is "such as" or just as it is.[8]

He goes on to say that "But if rightness (truth) of statement is only made possible by the overt character of behaviour, then it follows that the thing that makes rightness possible in the first place must have a more original claim to be regarded as the essence of truth."[9] Albert Hofstadter sums up approvingly Heidegger's understanding of the conventional correspondence concept of truth as an "uncovering" in these terms: "We might therefore say that statement, as such, articulates a human aiming at what-is. This aiming is an attempt at or an effort after the uncovering of what-is. If the effort succeeds, so that the intended entity is selfsame with the real entity, the statement is true. It uncovers the entity; the intention, transcending itself, reaches its destination; or *vice versa*, on reaching its destination, it uncovers the entity, bringing it into the openness of human being."[10]

Heidegger's truth as an "uncovering" not only is perhaps best exemplified in his understanding of art, but finds there its clearest articulation. In his "poetic" description of a peasant woman's shoes in Van Gogh's famous painting, Heidegger says: "From the dark opening of the worn insides of the shoes the toilsome tread of the worker stares forth. In the stiffly rugged heaviness of the shoes there is the accumulated tenacity of her slow trudge through the far-spreading and ever-uniform furrows of the field swept by a raw wind. On the leather lie the dampness and richness of the soil. Under the shoes vibrates the silent call of the earth, its quiet gift of ripening grain."[11] He then allows that

> Van Gogh's painting is the disclosure of what the equipment, the pair of peasant shoes, *is* in truth. This entity emerges into the unconcealedness of its being. . . .
>
> In the work of art the truth of an entity has set itself to work. 'To set' means here: to bring to a stand. Some particular entity, a pair of peasant shoes, comes in the work to stand in the light of its being. The being of the being comes into the steadiness of its shining.
>
> The nature of art would then be this: the truth of beings setting itself to work.[12]

After dismissing a copy view of art ("Van Gogh's work does not depict a pair of actually existing peasant shoes") Heidegger asserts that the work is "the reproduction of the thing's general essence" and asks, "Where does a work of art belong?" He answers, "The work belongs as work, uniquely within the realm that is opened up by itself."

Now, for all of Heidegger's striking originality, it does not seem that his general conception of truth and its further articulation in his thinking about art is a radical breaking away from the "correspondence" tradition. He is, it seems, looking more for the "essence" of the conventional sense of truth rather than developing a thorough-going notion of "rightness" that can encompass both statement truth and truth in art within a more generalized conceptual framework. Mehta acknowledges as much when he says that the "interpretation of truth as being discovering is neither arbitrary nor does it throw overboard the good old tradition, as it might at first appear, but is only the necessary explication of what was foreshadowed in it."[13]

We need, I think, to look clearly, and as deeply as we can, into the manner in which artworks are able to achieve a rightness, a truth that is appropriate to their own intentionality as art. The thesis that I will argue (in the spirit, if not the word, of Heidegger) is that *a work of art is true when and only when it attains authenticity through the presentation of its own intentionality.*

Authenticity

A work of art is authentic when it has a dynamic completeness that is natural and proper to it. Authenticity in art means the exhibiting of a unique wholeness, presenting the object in and through its own conditions of existence. A work of art must always be in some medium (a poem must be in at least *a* language), with the medium imposing a variety of restraints on and opportunities for the work: A work of art, like a person, has its accidents of birth, its specific (historical) time and (cultural) place, with all the existential conditions (e.g., technical means available, cultural expectations and values, accepted "vocabularies," and modes of representation) that these imply. A work of art that is authentic appears to affirm itself by acknowledging these conditions.

And this acknowledgment means something more that the artwork's simply fulfilling or showing its conditions. An artwork that is only the fulfillment of its conditions becomes utterly clear, and thereby uninteresting; it becomes only an *example* or *instance* that is explainable by its conditions (e.g., an inferior work of any particular "school"). Authenticity in art calls for creative uniqueness; which is to say that the dynamic completeness natural and proper to a work of art must always be irreplaceable. The artwork must acknowledge its conditions in the fullest sense of working with, but through, them to the realization of a special wholeness or unique integrity.

Integrity suggests strength and confidence. An integral artwork or realized person has no need of pretense. It is impossible "to fake it" in art, for although there may be fakes and forgeries, no work of art can survive the awareness that it is not really what it presents itself (pretends) to be. An artwork is an *exposed* being. It is highly vulnerable to a penetrating aesthetic consciousness. We readily, in most cases almost immediately, recognize the inauthentic—and reject it.

But when a work of art has integrity we accept the work for what it is. We affirm its being as being right for itself. "We expect a work of art to convince us," writes Dorothy Walsh, "but not by argument and not by evidence. Its authenticity must be internal to its concrete sensual presence. Given this authenticity, we accept it."[14]

We are not likely to apprehend a work of art as authentic or true and at the same time disvalue it aesthetically. For truth is not something that is superadded to (or subtractable from) the formal qualities of the work. Nevertheless, aesthetically there is more to the artwork than its truth, so that it does not follow that we necessarily ascribe "greatness" to a work that is true. (Truth in art is a necessary but not sufficient condition for excellence.) We may find the true artwork to lack an adequate depth of power, meaning, and radiance, but because of its integrity, its self-sufficiency, we advance no mental alternatives to its presentation.

Now a work of art has, of course, alternatives: in the sense of there being other possibilities for it entirely, there are an unlimited number; but when the work is true we recognize that it is right for itself, that it is *necessary* as it is. As Albert Hofstadter notes, "What is right, necessary, and an end in itself is what has attained to truth of being, i.e., to a condition of being in which it is as it ought to be in terms of its own ought."[15]

When we speak of "necessity" in art, we do so it seems always in the context of our recognizing the work as a created thing, one that is open to infinite possibilities; or to put it another way, one whose being is self-determined. As we have noted before, in contrast to our experience of "design" in natural objects, where we recognize that the necessity governing the design is external, as it were, to it (the flower designwise is what it is in terms of its being a particular expression or concentration of indifferent, universal forces and principles; it is a *product* of those forces), in our experience of artworks we discern (quite unconsciously and unthinkingly no doubt) its freedom precisely as self-determination. Its rightness is *inherent*; it does not follow from natural laws but from the dynamic interactions of its elements as controlled by the creative intelligence of its maker. The artwork is thus discerned by us in its full uniqueness as it is itself a world of intended meaning.

Own Intentionality

Judgments concerning rightness do take place within a context of our recognizing possibilities, within what I would like to call, following (while substantially revising) Hofstadter, an *intention*. "In order that a thing should be objectively true, it must possess for itself the intention or concept which is in conformity with the thing's realized existence and it must realize this intention in its existence. The thing must be one whose being, as a thing, is a realization of its *own* intention and whose *own* intention uncovers itself eventually as what it is. A true thing must be a self-attaining nisus toward a truth that is the truth of its own being."[16]

"Intention" is a difficult notion and one subject to a good deal of misunderstanding. To clear away one problem immediately, I do not mean that judgments about truth in art require us to know the intention of the artist (an artist seldom has a simple, identifiable, preconceived intention that is as such subsequently realized in the work; his or her intention, rather, is brought forth in the work during its making). I mean that any work of art intends its own mode of being; it has its own essential character as a work of art, its drive to be the thing that is right for it.

The locus of intentionality, I want to argue, is the artwork itself. The intentionality of any thing is what the thing itself aims to be by its own nature, which aim, however, is not an abstract ideal (a projected model or externally imposed idea of perfection) nor a preexistent form (a latent idea or potentiality) of the thing but that inherent power of the thing to give rise to the conditions under which its own authenticity is discerned. The intentionality of a thing is that drive of the thing to become what it ought to become according to its own process of development. An intentionality is thus an immanent objective of a being in process. It is that which autochthonously sets the standard for itself and the kind of thing that it is.

Now, the intentionality of a thing as a "drive to become what it ought to become" is not, of course, to be taken literally in the sense that the object (the artwork) is assumed to have a volitional capacity, as do human beings. The intentionality of an artwork is clearly imparted to it by human beings. But still there is very real sense in our speaking as if artworks had the capacity to realize their intentionality in a primary way, for one of the most interesting things about artworks is their tendency to have a life of their own; which is to say that once in process they go autogenetically to influence their own development and, in turn, to contribute to the development of the maker of them.

The term *intentionality* has come into prominence in contemporary philosophy through phenomenology. Following Franz Brentano, who, in his *Psychologie vom empirischen Standpunkt* of 1874, distinguished "psychical phenomena" from "physical phenomena" according as the former has the characteristic of always referring to a content, as containing within itself an immanent objectlike entity, whether existing objectively or not, Husserl developed the idea of the intentionality of consciousness, that consciousness, by its nature, is always consciousness *of* an object. An intention is constituted *in* consciousness.[17]

Phenomenology thus uses "intentionality" as the characteristic way in which consciousness functions in relation to its world, the way, that is, in which mental acts present the subject with an object. I see no reason, however, to restrict "intentionality" to human consciousness, for the immanent objectivity that I am concerned to identify (and hence my very use of the term) is, as I see it, a characteristic feature of entities like artworks and various language types, as indeed of human beings themselves.

Intentionality, as I use the term, refers to the aiming for particularized expression that is intrinsic to the being of anything capable of realizing an intrinsic meaningfulness. The intentionality of a thing is not its "concept" (Hegel's *Begriff,* as Hofstadter seems to suggest); rather it is the particularized concern of the thing to be what it ought to be, with the *ought* itself dynamically established in terms of the special circumstances of the individual thing.

And when something is properly realized we discern its rightness, its authenticity, precisely as the articulation of its intentionality. To articulate an intentionality means to realize explcitly the thing's own aim to be. The realization is within the matrix of the existential conditions of the thing, and it is, necessarily, a dynamic realization. The articulated, as we have seen, is not just a finished thing; rather, it is the thing as always open to our discerning new meanings and values in it, to its being "corrected" in the light of new experience.

Art, I have argued, intends to be aesthetically forceful, meaningful, and beautiful. The intention of a particular work of art, therefore, is precisely its drive to realize this intentionality under the artwork's own existential conditions. A work of art, in other words, strives to be the *unique* thing that is right for it within the framework of the intentionality of art.

Paul Klee's *Die Heilige vom innern Licht* is true. It is aesthetically forceful, meaningful, and beautiful just in its own way as a dynamic completeness that is natural and proper to it. It is a right presentation or articulation of its own intentionality.

Thematically one might ask, Who is the "holy one" here? Where is he? Why is he holy? In the *Theologia Germanica*, an anonymous mystical work of the fourteenth century, we read: "Now the created soul of man . . . has two eyes. The one is the power of seeing into eternity, the other of seeing into time and the creatures, of perceiving how they differ from each other. . . . But these two eyes of the soul of man cannot perform their work at once; but if the soul shall see with the right eye into eternity, then the left eye must cease and refrain from all its working, and be as though it were dead."[18]

The "created soul of man," we are told, cannot at once see the eternal and the temporal and consequently is self-divided. The "holy one," the soul of man, Klee is telling us as well, is a sea of infinite possibility. It can be involved completely in the world or it can reach for a joyful self-transcending contemplation.

Now, we may reject this metaphysics and assert, for example, that there is no "other world" at all or that such a world can indeed be wholly immanent in our experience, but the truth of the artwork is not judged by this criterion. Truth in art does not requires an assent to the worldview or philosophy that might be suggested by or be "embodied" in the work. A work of art is not true *to* something else—its truth is not dependent on its meaning being translated into propositions or statements that correspond with or to some state of affairs external to it—rather, its truth, like its meaning, is inherent in it. Klee's work has integrity; its vision is articulated rightly with aesthetic force, meaning, and beauty—and that is enough. We may disagree with the view presupposed in or suggested by it, but we cannot rightfully disagree with the work aesthetically because of its view.[19] We recognize aesthetically its authority and authenticity, its powerful manner of affirming itself. There is a masterful certainty in the line delineating the figure; the means of lithography are employed with integrity; the subdued coloration is entirely appropriate—in short, the work does compel our like-mindedness. *Die Helige von innern Licht* is authentic; but one would not

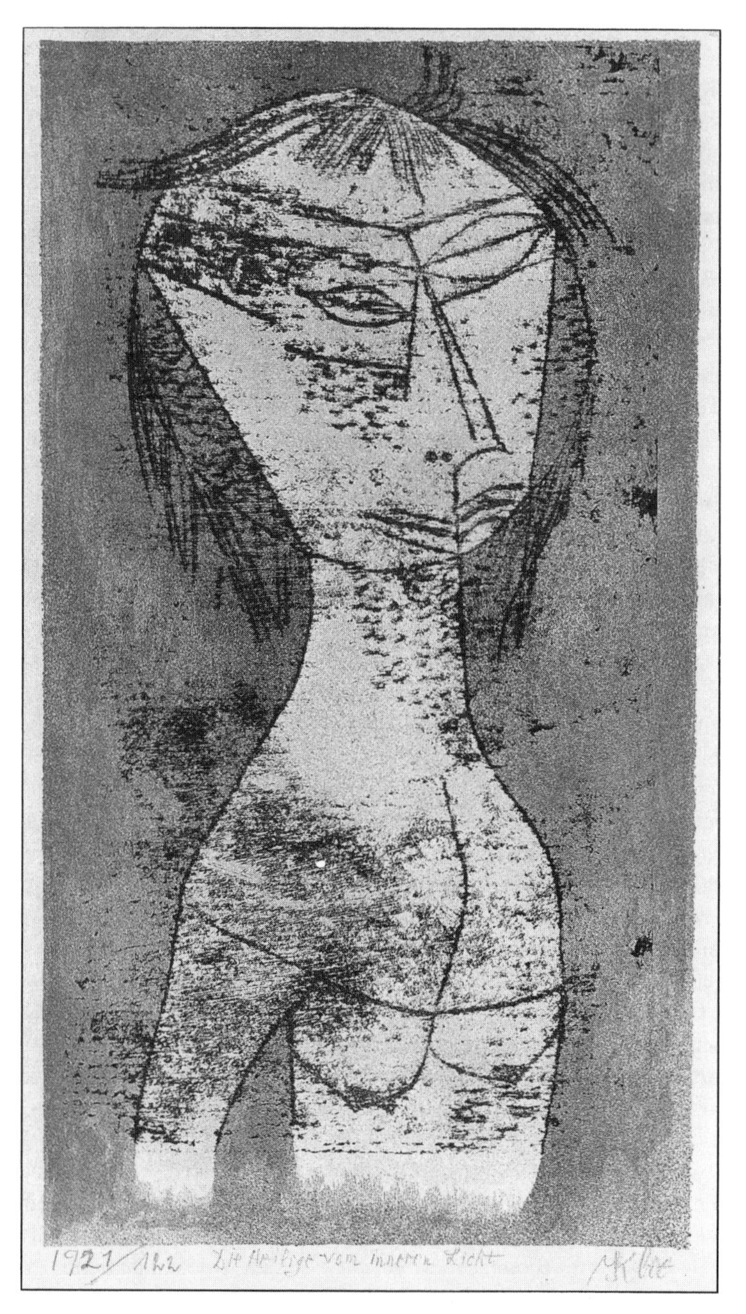

Figure 12.1. Paul Klee (Swiss 1879–1940). *The Saint of the Inner Light*, 1921. Lithograph in three colors on German paper. 12-3/16 x 6-13/16 inches (53.46). The Norton Simon Museum

say that it is "perfect." Perfection in art (which too often involves just a static completeness) may in fact lead to falsity, to that which is unnatural and inappropriate in the object that bears it.

Salvador Dali's *Crucifixion* (originally entitled *Corpus hipercubus* or *Hypercubic Body* by the artist) has a kind of perfection, but it lacks integrity. Although Chester Dale, who donated the work to New York City's Metropolitan Museum of Art, claims that "it is a very honest picture, very great,"[20] one cannot but discern the disparity between the advertisinglike qualities of the painting, with its unsymbolic cross constructed of floating cubes and its alleged symbolic values. There exists here an enormous gap between intention and pretension. The grandly robed figure at the lower left (said to be modeled by Dali's wife) is insipid (and quite dispensable). The work is an unchristian (and not even anti- or postchristian) crucifixion, which is to say that it is inauthentic. The work does not achieve a dynamic wholeness through the acknowledgment of its existential conditions. It is artificial and thus lacks integrity.

We contradict, we falsify, in art when we recognize that the artwork needs to be replaced in its own being with another possibility that would be right for it. We falsify (weakly) when we recognize unrealized potentiality; we falsify (strongly) when we recognize inauthentic realization; when, as with Dali's work, we recognize pretense, when we fail to find reality.

When the artwork is true, as with Klee's work, it has the aesthetic force, the inherent significance, the internal necessity, the rightness that exhibits strength and confidence and that calls for acceptance and assent to its being.

* * *

In discussing various criticisms of the traditional "coherence" theory of truth, Alan White writes, "It is no objection to the truth of a statement in a particular mathematical system that there are or may be other systems with whose members it does not cohere. . . . [It] is logically possible to have two different but equally comprehensive sets of coherent statements . . ."[21] What is logically possible for mathematics is, we might say, empirically necessary for art. One true work of art does not stand in competition with another work that is true. The truth of one work of art does not require the falsity of another work. The untrue is simply the unrealized and the inauthentic.

* * *

This brings us to one of the most difficult problems for the theme of truth in art—the matter of forgeries.[22] There seems to be something very puzzling about a situation where an artwork is first experienced as a great work of art (or at least is regarded as great) by those considered to be best qualified to make the judgment (e.g., the Vermeer experts in relation to the famous Van Meergeren forgeries) and then without the artwork's undergoing any change in itself, on learning that it is a forgery, it is rejected and disvalued by the experts and by others who follow their judgments. We think somehow that the forgery ought still to be the cause of a satisfying experience if indeed it had that capability in the first place. We are ready to admit that its economic value might rightfully change, but we do not see how there can rightfully be a change in its aesthetic value.

The view of truth in art that I have tried to state can, I think, deal most effectively with this problem; for, in the simplest terms, the recognition of an artwork's inauthenticity (in this case the clear recognition of the disparity between the object as it is and as it, through another, claims to be) is precisely a basis for rejecting it. Our knowledge about what a thing is necessarily enters into our perception (interpretation, evaluation) of it. The forgery does not rightfully affirm its existential conditions (this is especially so when a contemporary artist manufactures a work for attribution to an artist of an entirely different period and cultural milieu), and hence it lacks truth. When controlled by the object, aesthetic experience is always more than just a formalist response to (isolable) formal qualities; for the aesthetic force, the significance and beauty of the work are inseparably present in the work as its structured content. We do not, in short, merely appreciate formal qualities of a certain kind apart from their having been produced in a particular way.[23]

We reject the forgery aesthetically, then, not because the work no longer conforms with (corresponds to) our idea of it (this would only trap us in that net of having the artwork be true to something external to it), but because the work is not true to itself. The forgery is inauthentic, and thus we are justified aesthetically in disvaluing it.[24]

And for the work that is true, as Alan White also notes, "A particular statement [or artwork] could be perfectly true without containing more than a minute portion of the whole truth even about a single topic. Being wholly true is not the same as being the whole truth."[25] The true work of art is a wholeness, but assuredly it is not the whole truth. The artworld consists of many presentations, some of which are right articulations of intentions that exhibit dynamic completeness. Some works of art are false and, happily, some are true.

13

Art and Morality

> There is no such thing as a moral or an immoral book. Books are well written or badly written. That is all.
>
> (Oscar Wilde)

> Even the most sublime work of art takes up a definite position *vis-à-vis* reality by stepping outside of reality's spell, not abstractly once and for all, but occasionally and in concrete ways, when it unconsciously and tacitly polemicizes against the condition of society at a particular point in time.
>
> (Theodor Adorno)

It is often thought today that there is an inherent and perhaps irreconcilable conflict between art and morality or between aesthetic and ethical consciousness. This conflict arises, it seems, from the recognition that, on the one hand, art and morality are kindred forms of spiritual life and, on the other, there are sharp differences between them and that, accordingly, they make opposing claims upon us. Sidney Zink sums up the sharp differences and opposing claims in these (not altogether adequate but) compact terms:

> Morality insists upon the interconnectedness of experiences; art insists upon the self-containedness of each particular experience. The moral man scrutinizes the given action for its relations to other actions; the aesthetic man absorbs himself in the immediate experience. Morality insists upon the inviolability of the man, art upon the inviolability of the experience. Morality recognizes the fact of dimensionality in life; art stresses the fact of qualitativeness. The first would make life consistent; the second would make it intense. Morality speaks in the interest of the whole, art in the interest of the part.[1]

Historically, of course, at other times and in other places, this way of characterizing art and morality would have been unintelligible. The dominant presupposition from the Hellenistic period to the Renaissance was simply that art was subservient to (or could in no way be separated from) the demands of morality, as theologically and politically defined and understood; and in traditional Asian cultures especially the relation between the moral quality of the artist as a person and the aesthetic quality of his work, as we will see, was thought to be intimate indeed.

Today, on the other hand, as we have noted, art has established its autonomy. Many (at least non-Marxist) aestheticians and critics today would even go so far as to say that the only "goodness" in art is of a strictly aesthetic kind. A work of art that is aesthetically right is simply "good" by virtue of this rightness—without moral remainder. We allow intrusions from the ethical into art only insofar as they can be taken over and entirely assimilated by purely aesthetic considerations. William H. Gass, for example, states that "it is the artist's task to add to the world objects and ideas—delineations, symphonies—which ought to be there, and whose end is contemplation and appreciation; things which deserve to become the focus of a truly disinterested affection. There is perhaps a moral in that."[2]

Plato and Tolstoy were perhaps the most articulate and historically important opponents of any view that upholds the radical autonomy of art and its separation from the ethical. According to Plato (*Ion, Phaedrus, Republic, Laws*) works of art appeal to the passional elements of the soul and, by the pleasure they afford, divert the souls's attention from rational contemplation, its proper end. Recognizing the efficacy of art to excite and stimulate the emotions, Plato would, in an ideal republic, ban artworks and artists who were intent on this excitement. Only those works that were conducive to fostering harmony and order in the soul would be tolerated.

Tolstoy, in his famous essay *What is Art?* wages the most thorough and sustained attack on a formalist view of art and its related *l'art pour l'art* standpoint. He insists that art does not have properly to do with "pleasure" so much as with the communication of feeling. And when the artwork is right, it has to do with communicating those feelings intimately related to the basic religious perception of the society; the perception for modern Western society having to do, so Tolstoy believed, with the universal brotherhood of man. Working from an (ill-developed) expression theory of art, Tolstoy argues that the artist has certain vivid feelings that are embodied in the work and then evoked in others. For the sake of "brotherhood" the cognitive (symbolic, intellectual) dimensions of art must be intelligible to the vast majority of humankind; it is the "everyman" in fact who discerns most clearly the natural accord between the feelings embodied in the artwork and genuine religiosity and morality.

Following Tolstoy, but in somewhat more contemporary Marxist terms, N. I. Bukharin argues: "Art is a means of 'socializing the feelings'. . . . The hearer of a musical work expressive of a certain mood will be 'infected,' permeated, with this mood; the feeling of the individual composer becomes the feeling of many persons, has been transferred to them, has 'influenced' them, a psychic state has been 'socialized'. The same holds good in any other art; painting, architecture, poetry, sculpture, etc."[3]

Now Plato's puritanism and Tolstoy's religious (and Bukarin's Marxist political) socialism are, we know, quite unacceptable. Plato neglects the revelatory powers of art and wrongly assumes that aesthetic satisfaction is of the same nature as body-based (noncognitive) sense pleasure. Tolstoy fails to understand the difference between the expression of various feelings in art and the creation in art of new forms of emotionality; and he fails to appreciate the distinction between complexities in art that are appropriate and those that are obscurantist.

It is interesting to observe in this context that historically it has been the totalitarian-minded political and the puritanical-oriented religious that have accorded to art the deepest social efficacy. Even though many modern artists (the Futurists, the members of the Bauhaus) certainly thought of their work as revolutionary, both in artistic and social terms, aestheticians and critics have nevertheless assumed that, with its purported universality, art was beyond interest-motivated politics and sectarian religious concerns. Totalitarian political thinking and practice, whether on the "left" or the "right," on the other hand, recognized the power of art to establish (a seditious) community and accordingly believed it to be highly dangerous. The "reading" of the art produced in this controlled context often became then an exercise more in decoding than in interpreting, in any interesting hermeneutic sense, and this became destructive of the very nature of art to show properly its formed content.[4]

With the puritanical religious, on the other hand, the antipathy toward art lay not so much in its power to mold subversive attitudes and values but, as noted, to drive one toward body-based sensuous pleasures, which bind one to one's lower nature and distract one from realizing one's higher nature. Art becomes the great tempter for one to re-enact the Fall.

In any event, both the totalitarian and the religious anti-art-as-autonomous attitudes are often quite mystifying to liberal thinking, which finds art to be among those private interests and activities that scarcely intrude upon the body politic, except when certain works depict subjects (usually sexual) offensive to large numbers of people. But even here, more often than not, and after tempers have cooled, the right to free expression asserts itself and art is once again "distanced" and regarded as harmless.

There ought, however, to be some middle ground where the social relevance of art (its power indeed to impact our lives) can be recognized without, on the one hand, being exaggerated so as to justify the control of art in the interests of a social ideology (and at times aesthetic know-nothingness) or, on the other hand, minimized to the point of public indifference, with art thereby becoming something essentially superfluous, a harmless luxury.

One way to establish this middle ground is first of all to distinguish clearly between those works of art that aspire to fulfill the intentionality of art (whether they succeed or not) from those works that clearly seek to promote a social attitude or ideology, whether mild (homespun values of motherhood and country) or offensive (racist, pornographic debasement) and are intended to be responded to primarily in terms of the bare "what" of their representation. The latter might be called simply *pseudo-art* (or propaganda or pornography masquerading as art). Genuine art, to a certain extent always immunizes its subject matter (insofar as it has one in the first place) through transforming it into aesthetic content; pseudo-art fails to (indeed, with its overwhelming didactic concerns, does not seek to) so transform its subject matter; rather it strives to state it as baldly as it can within the constraints and opportunities of aesthetic stylization so as to magnify just those life reactions associated with it. In short, it is only pseudo-art that the totalitarian and the religious may rightfully find congenial to their own concerns.

A genuine work of art, then, is never, as the totalitarian political and the puritanical religious would have us believe, a proposition, statement, or argument clothed in the form of art. It is rather sui generis; its moral dimension is embedded in the totality that is the work.

Now various moral beliefs or ethical attitudes, of course, can be set forth in an artwork through the voices of different characters (especially in literature and drama) or through subject-matter depictions in the visual arts (e.g., massacres and the like) without these representing or expressing the moral stance of the artist. Indeed literary critics often distinguish the authorial voice in a work from the voice of the writer as such, with the possibility then obtaining that the former does not speak for the latter, but only, as it were, for the work itself, the writer remaining thereby untouched by what is said. Milan Kundera states that

> on lending himself to the role of public figure, the novelist endangers his work; it risks being considered a mere appendage to his actions, to his declarations, to his statements of position. Now, not only is the novelist nobody's spokesman, but I would go so far as to say that he is not even the spokesman for his own ideas. When Tolstoy sketched the first draft of *Anna Karenina*, Anna was a most unsympathetic woman, and her tragic end was entirely deserved and justified. The final version of the novel is very different, but I do not believe that Tolstoy had revised his moral ideas in the meantime; I would say, rather, that in the course of writing, he was listening to aanother voice than that of his personal moral conviction.[5]

But this can clearly be taken too far if it means that only when the two are identical (the writer speaking exclusively in the first person as his or her person) can judgment of a moral sort be made with respect to the writer; for under any circumstances the writer is responsible for his or her choice of authorial voice and need be mindful of its social impact. Kundera himself goes on to note that "Every novel, like it or not, offers some answer to the question: What is human existence, and wherein does its poetry lie?"[6]

Also in many instances the artist does present in his or her work, and affirms elsewhere when talking about it, a clearly identified moral or political viewpoint that may be repugnant to most persons (a Céline, an Ezra Pound). Although when responding to the viewpoint set forth in the work we inevitably respond to it as it is embedded there, which is to say as it is interwoven with the manner of the entire work's presentational efficacy, otherwise the work would not be an artwork but a moral treatise or political tract, we do recognize the viewpoint for what it is and are compelled thereby to engage it. The moral responsibility of the artist for what he or she presents is here obviously intense.[7]

But neither the placing of art under "morality" and making it subservient to political or religious ends nor the insisting on the utter exclusion of the moral from art (nor the seeking of the kind of "middle ground" outlined previously) is, of course, the only way by which the alleged conflict between art and morality can be and has been adjudicated. Kant, with his notion that "the beautiful is the symbol of the morally good" and that "the mind is made conscious of a certain ennoblement and elevation above the mere sensibility to pleasure received through sense,"[8] for example, tries to give some content, however thin, to the idea of a possible perfect accord obtaining between the ethical and the aesthetic; in other words, to the idea that, based on the spectator's mind being ennobled through its experience of the beautiful, there need be no essential conflict between them.

But this hardly accords with much modern (post-Kantian) experience where the emphasis has shifted from our experience of "the beautiful" (and for Kant this meant primarily our experience of beauty in nature) to that of our experience of the full intentionality of art, where "beauty," in Kant's sense, as we have seen, is of negligible importance.[9]

Croce also looks for a straightforward resolution of the problem, but unlike Kant, he looks to the artist rather than to the spectator. He writes,

> The basis of all poetry [art] is human personality, and, since human personality finds its completion in morality, the basis of all poetry is the moral consciousness. Of course this does not mean that the artist must be a profound thinker or an acute critic; not that he must be a pattern of virtue or a hero; but he must have a share in the world of thought and action which will enable him, either in his own person or by sympathy with others, to live the whole drama of human life.[10]

But the artist's having "a share in the world of thought and action" (does anyone *not* have such a share?) is clearly insufficient to resolve the problem of determining the moral dimension of art within the framework of art's own required autonomy. We can perhaps get some help in the resolution of this problem by turning briefly to some selected aspects of traditional Asian thought.

In *An Essay on Landscape Painting* (*Lin Ch'üan Kao Chih*), Kuo Hsi, an eleventh-century painter and writer, sets forth the typical Chinese view: "[If the artist] can develop a natural, sincere, gentle and honest heart, then he will immediately be able to comprehend the aspects of tears and smiles and of objects, pointed or oblique, bent or inclined, and they will be so clear in his mind that he will able to put them down spontaneously with his paint brush."[11] He goes on to say, "When I am responsive and at one with my surroundings and have achieved perfect coordination of mind and hand, then I start to paint freely and expertly, as the proper standard of art demands."[12]

The state of being of the artist, Kuo Hsi maintains, is always reflected ("embodied") in his or her work. Who the artist is as a (moral, spiritual) person will always show in his or her work. It is not then just that an artist may (or may not) present a moral viewpoint (as a set of beliefs or claims), rather one inevitably will be disclosed in one's work as the kind of person one is. For the Chinese, the style of the work and the style of the artist are, if not entirely coincident, never radically separable.

Indian aesthetics, too, has this keen sense of the intimate relations that obtain between the being of the artist and the quality of his or her work. The entire creative act is traditionally understood (in somewhat more extensive metaphysical terms than the Chinese) as a natural extension of a spiritual process. The artist, it is often said, must be a kind of *karmayogīn*, one who acts without attachment to the fruits of one's action and in a manner of loving concern or devotion (*bhakti*) that is informed by knowledge or awareness (*jñāna*) of what is real and valuable. For traditional Indian aesthetics, genuine creativity is thus an illusion making that is conscious of itself. The artist must, if he or she is to act in play (*līlā*, activity carried out for its own sake), be aware of both sides, as it were, of the great ontological divide: The artist must work *with* the materials of his or her art (*māyā*) from the nonobsessive stance that comes from the achievement of nonegocentricity, the realization of the self. And the *rasika*, one who experiences rightly the *rasa*, is called on in traditional Indian aesthetics to be a *sahṛdaya*, one of similar heart; he or she must be equal to the work in his or her own achieved sensitivity in order to experience the work properly. The spectator, as well then as the artist, finds the moral and the aesthetic to be as one.

But, one may well ask, what does this non-Western confounding of the moral and the aesthetic have to do with the problem at hand, which is that of locating the moral dimension of art within the context of what we understand today to be the autonomy of art? What we can learn from the traditional Asian views, I think, as it bears on our problem today, is fundamentally this: Creativity, and thus art, by its nature, is celebrative and calls for a loving consciousness.

Creativity, I would argue, always manifests concern; and thus by its very nature, art is a celebration of personhood and world, if not in their given actualities at least in their (real) potentialities. A Goya *Disasters of War*, a Grünewald *Crucifixion*, Picasso's *Guernica* are affirmative, for they point to and take their judgmental stand from a concern for human dignity and worth. An artist overcome by dejection, by despair and agony, could not create. He or she might be able to shout and scream, as others might do, although more likely the artist would sink into apathy and hopelessness; in any event "being overcome" is not conducive to creativity and indeed is incompatible with it.

Recognizing the immense cruelty often exhibited by one's fellow human beings, and perhaps as well the capacity for cruelty in oneself ("Saint Genet"); seeing the gross stupidity, selfishness, and perversity—the evil, in short—that seems always to intrude into human affairs; being aware of that nothingness, the obliteration, that appears finally to render all human achievements futile, the artist, nevertheless, as artist, possesses that loving consciousness which acknowledges an intrinsic value to self and other. For without that acknowledgment one would not be able to recognize, as indeed one must, the possibility of creating worth and value in the truth and beauty that is to be there in the work. Art cannot help but be celebrative.

The positive moral dimension of art as art has nothing directly to do, then, with the "motive" of the artist or with his or her moral or political viewpoint or ethical "virtue" as such.[13] It has to do only with that special lovingness which informs imagination and intuition and that is at the heart of artistic creativity. This love, this concern, this celebration resounds in the work and demands our openness to it. In at least this sense, then, all genuine art is inherently moral. And it affords the grounding of art in social community.

While it is certainly the case that art, in virtue of its being for consciousness, is necessarily communal in character and thus, for its understanding and appreciation, can never be divorced completely from its social context,[14] it is the celebrative quality of art that grounds the truth of Dewey's observation that "In the end, works of art are the only media of complete and unhindered communication between man and man that can occur in a world full of gulfs and walls that limit community of experience."[15] *Community* means a coming together through shared values and interests. This "coming together" takes place not only in obvious audience situations, where as a participant with others we become united in a common intention and expectation and conform our behavior to the demands of the situation, but also in those creating and experiencing moments of intense aloneness, for these are thoroughly informed by a sense of a sharing that is yet to be; a reaching out to others in and through the celebrative art-making and aesthetic experience. A communion to be established with others is always implicit in all art making and experience.

Schiller, in the play theory of art that he sets forth in *On the Aesthetic Education of Man* (1795), argues that "taste alone brings harmony into society, because it fosters harmony in the individual." For Schiller, the moral dimension of art to foster "harmony" is intrinsic to it and is not a "function" to be imposed on it. Art by its nature points to community, even when it intends, for a specific political purpose, to be subversive. Arguing from a feminist perspective, Rita Zelski writes that "it is not the text which reflects female experience that best serves feminist interests, but rather the work which disrupts the very structures of symbolic discourse through which patriarchal culture is constituted."[16] A politics of art that seeks to emancipate female experience and interests from a structure of discourse guided by, and informed throughout, by male experience and interests nevertheless clearly does strive for a form of liberated community. It thus recognizes, in the last analysis, that the powers of art, being celebratory, are essentially spiritual and not narrowly political. The very community the subversive feminist artist is intent upon creating is permeated with moral concern.

Gadamer has observed that "The artist no longer speaks for the community, but forms his own community insofar as he expresses himself. Nevertheless, he does create a community, and in principle, this truly universal community (oikumene) extends to the whole world."[17]

It is precisely this "extension" from narrower to larger social contexts that Confucianism traditionally sees as the appropriate way for an individual to be as a moral, social person. The role of the work of art in building community starts from a local situation, a specific time and place, and then reaches out to a contemporary audience within one's culture, extending then to those from other cultures, and finally, if it endures, to other generations. Even the Marxist literary critic Gyorgy Lukács can write that "Men experience in great works of art the present and past of humanity, perspectives on its development. They experience them, however, not as external facts which one may acknowledge as more or less important, but as something essential for one's own life, as an important moment also of one's own individual existence."[18] If, as some philosophers (Taylor, MacIntyre) claim, a person is and is able to become such, only as he or she is a member of various communities and traditions, then quite clearly art more than any other human endeavor makes this possible. Our experience of artworks enables us to enter cultures, times, and places other than our own and eventually to appropriate them precisely as our own and thereby to extend the self into an ever-widening community of humankind.

14

Religion and Art

Religion and art stand beside each other like two friendly souls whose inner relationship, if they suspect it, is still unknown to them.
(Schleiermacher)

Giovanni Bellini and Saint Francis

Saint Francis is wholly in and out of relation to Nature. The realm of Grace is nowhere explicitly represented, yet there is no doubt that Saint Francis is intimately involved with it. It is as though he were trying to bring everything in Nature along with him: The rocks and trees, birds and beasts, that are bathed in a pale blue glow, are being carried, through the power of his joy, to the colorless Divine; though they are indifferent to or are unaware of it.

Saint Francis is a part of Nature. He does not stand out from it by virtue of any pronounced position he occupies in the composition; yet it is clear that he is superior to Nature because of his ecstasy. He transcends Nature and, by transcending, celebrates it.

"No other great painting," writes Kenneth Clark, "perhaps contains such a quantity of natural details, observed and rendered with incredible patience: for no other painter has been able to give such an accumulation the unity which is only achieved by love."[1] Bellini's love and Saint Francis's love are here the same. Their love is that joyous affirmation which is grounded in the depth of humility; it is that delicate feeling which brings a simple harmony to a rich complexity; it is that integrity which encompasses and transforms whatever it embraces. Yet there is a disquieting note. A subtle tension exists between this human love and that which is thought to be gracious. The love is unqualified, but can we be confident that it is being accepted by the hidden Divine? It is what is literally absent here, rather than what is present as such, that gives the work its tremendous excitement and suspense.

Figure 14.1.
Giovanni Bellini.
St. Francis in the Desert.
Copyright The Frick Collection, New York

The book on the reading table is closed, for what use has Saint Francis for language? Language enables him to go beyond the temporal present; it carries him back to the past and forward to the future and makes everything present to him. But language is time bound and ecstasy is timeless.

The donkey is in *the present. His consciousness is momentary; it is exhausted by its experience at hand. Saint Francis* is *the present, the Now that contains and transcends all temporality. Yet, Saint Francis has a history. The skull on the table is his destiny, too.*

Are Bellini and Saint Francis interchangeable? Can the artist be a saint or the saint an artist?

Bellini desires perfection for his work; Saint Francis, that state of being which for him is alone perfect.

Saint Francis needs that eternal silence which extinguishes all sound; Bellini, that sound, that life which inspires growth and change.

Bellini must be involved with contrasts and with particular things in their unique particularity, and he must exhibit this involvement in his work. Saint Francis must care for nothing so little as to draw attention to something he may create. His sole concern is to draw attention to the silent Divine; to that which ultimately is without contrast or form.

Bellini and Saint Francis are not interchangeable. The artist and the saint cannot do each other's work.

Homo religiosus is now secondary to, but nevertheless aligned with, *homo faber* as *poietis*. Let us look more closely at some of the relationships between them.

The Making of a Religion-Work

Let us, to begin with, define a religion-work, as distinct from a *religious work* of art, as a specific rite, hymn, dance, or other symbolic form whose primary function is to lead the participant in it to a distinctive religious state of being, as this state may be defined in a particular religious tradition. With the religion-work, in contrast to an artwork, aesthetic contemplation and enjoyment is by intention secondary to this primary function of "leading to". The religion-work, in short, does not intend to be an expressive form—to be aesthetically forceful, meaningful and beautiful—although it might coincidentally lend itself to being responded to in a manner appropriate to fulfilling that intentionality; it intends rather to be "magical." A religion-work has a *ritual* function designed to bring about new relationships between persons(s) and the sacred, to be a means for the transformation of self.

Who creates a religion-work? The answer must be that in most cases it is impossible to specify an individual maker of this kind of work. Try to imagine a particular person deciding to create a religion-work the way a Rembrandt may decide to set up his easel and work on his painting. Religion-works seem to be group expressions that have arisen organically, as it were, in the context of cult needs. They are expressive of a collective will, not of an individual genius.[2]

The participant in a religion-work is therefore part of the creative process that brings it into active being. Without her the ritual is a lifeless, empty form. The participant, though, it must be understood, is not just another individual qua (subjective) individual in the sense that one would be performing a private ritual. A ritual may be performed in private, but (like a Wittgensteinian understanding of language) it demands always a public context or rule-based group identity. Without the cult we do not have a ritual, we have an obsessional neurosis.

The participant in a religion-work feels that the object (the spiritual power, the god) to which the work is "dedicated" is present in the work and, in this somewhat paradoxical way, that the work generates the presence. When the participatory-making of the work is completed, like with "primitive" religious consciousness generally, the power, it is believed, withdraws and is there only latently. In contrast to the artist's exciting sense of *discovery*, as Eliade and others have convincingly shown, the creative participant in the religion-work has an awesome awareness of *recovery*. The (modern) artist feels that one is bringing something new into being; the participant in the religion-work that one is re-enacting a timeless possibility.

The religion-work, however, like the artwork, does embody a kind of play. It calls for a special role playing or acting, one that, from the standpoint of the participant-maker, must be entirely unself-conscious. The role playing, to be right for itself, must be a complete stepping-out (*ekstasis*) from one's ordinary functional life; one must actually become the role during the time of the play. And this is perhaps why so few of us today are capable any longer of being full participant-makers of religion-works. We are fearful of losing ourselves in the intense self-giving required. We are afraid that with the abandonment of "self-control" we may encounter only the demonic.

In art, the play must be entirely natural to the artist; that is to say, it must be a spontaneous, albeit highly disciplined, expression and articulation of one's being. In religion, the play must be as a cosmic offering, with the player being utterly forgetful of one's own being. Sacramentally, a religion-work is a solemn "sacrifice."

Art as Religious, Religion as Aesthetic

Both art and religion may be revelatory of being. Each, in its way, may present something of the spiritual life for response and appropriation; each may articulate intuitions of spiritual being. What makes a work of art religious? Many works of art are said to be religious in virtue of their subject matter, in virtue of what they are "about." The subject matter of an artwork must, however, as much modern aesthetics insists, be distinguished from the aesthetic meaning or the proper content of the work. Albert Hofstadter draws the distinction nicely in this way:

> It is helpful to distinguish between content in the sense of material or subject-matter included in the artistically constructed figure and content in the sense of the particular meaning of the work itself, for the expression of which the materials and subject-matters are brought into it. A landscape painter includes a rock, a pond, and trees in his paintings. They are materials, subject-matters, introduced into the artistic composition for the sake of making the figure. The figure as a whole is the total composition itself—the landscape, as such, is the meaning that belongs to it as just that total artistic composition.[3]

The subject matter of an artwork is what the elements in the work may be said to refer to (Saint Francis, the donkey and birds, the wilderness) or what the work as a whole may, if it is appropriate, be "about" (Saint Francis ecstatically in the wilderness). The meaning, the content in the proper sense, of the artwork is the formed unity of the particular work itself as it embodies and conveys a unique concrete meaning or intuition of being. The artwork, on this account, then, is religious when that concrete intuition is of spiritual being. Religious art is not simply art that has religion as its subject matter. The representation of the Crucifixion, of a meditating Buddha, or the inclusion of clearly identifiable symbols of whatever religious tradition by itself constitutes what some people call *religious art*, but it is "religious" only at its most transparent, purely nominal, and aesthetically uninteresting level.

Here, of course, the battle between art and religion over the obligation of art to conform to theology has often been fought. And the conflict is not just an historical curiosity. As sophisticated and prominent a modern thinker as Jacques Maritain can still write that "Sacred [religious] art is in a state of absolute dependence upon theological wisdom. There is manifested in the figure it sets before our eyes something far above all our human art, divine truth itself, the treasure of light purchased for us by the blood of Christ. For this reason chiefly, because the sovereign interests of the Faith are at stake in the matter, the Church exercises its authority and magistracy over sacred art."[4]

But art, like language, is sacred, as it were, only insofar as it is revelatory of spiritual being; only insofar, that is, as it radiates with an intuition of spiritual being. Maritain confounds a whole type of artwork with religion proper and refuses thereby to acknowledge the emergence of the artwork as an autonomous form of spiritual life. Hofstadter writes,

> Religion interprets reality by means of symbols and rituals that depend only in part upon their expressive appearances to communicate their meanings.

> The consecrated wafer does not need to look like the body of God. Its religious potency and meaning depend more on representational connections in the mind, often quite independent of the symbol, then on its actual aspect. . . .
>
> What art does is to articulate an image which exists as the object of intuition and which gives to intuition an immediate grasp of meaning.[5]

The religious dimension of the artwork rests, then, precisely on that articulation of "an image which exists as the object of intuition," when that intuition is of the essential order of being.

* * *

Turning now to the other side of the kinship between art and religion, *the aesthetic dimension of religion* is often taken to consist in a spectator's disinterested (nonparticipating) appreciation of a religious ceremony or religion-work of whatever kind as an aesthetic object—as if the religion-work, in formal terms, were a kind of artwork (e.g., Santayana). Now, it is, of course, possible to adopt this "aesthetic attitude" to anything whatever and it is, of course, true that religion-works frequently contain formal qualities that lend themselves to aesthetic appreciation quite readily, but it should also be clear enough that one who is seeking aesthetic qualities per se is better advised to look for them in their primary place with their full expressive potentiality, namely, in works of art, and that one would be well advised to look for the aesthetic dimension of the religion-work at a somewhat deeper level of experience. This level, I believe, is one that involves us once again in symbol and meaning.

Hofstadter, as we pointed out before, separated religion from art by placing the former in the domain of conventional symbolic values. But this is too strong a separation; for if it were so, no one would respond to a religion-work religiously, but only cognitively—with, to be sure, the various emotive factors that accompany any cognitive concern. The conventional symbolic is, we would agree, dominant in religion, but it is effective religiously only insofar as it is allied with, at one end, the magic power associated with the "primitive" and, at the other end, with the spiritual meaning of art itself.

I have pointed out before that in the historical relationship between art and religion, there is a primal stage where no distinction is drawn between art and religion.[6] At this stage we have art religion-works that engender and express what is taken to be a magical power or efficacy. The value of the religion-work, once the separation between art and religion occurs, will thus lay for many persons precisely in the degree to which this power engendering is still thought to be present in it—a power engendered, not by symbolic meanings as such, but by patterns and movements, gestures and sounds, invested with magical potency.

At the other end, the religion-work (e.g., the Mass) is responded to, is participated in, religiously because of the degree to which it may be "a form that articulates a meaning for intuition," that is to say, the degree to which the conventional symbolic meanings are made alive by the presence of essentiality embedded in the work. The conventional symbolic—with the symbols being commensurate with the theology of the particular tradition—is the subject matter of the work and also its dominant content; but the work itself, at this end of the spectrum, is for a participant a religion-work and not just a bare conveyor of symbols. With genuine, living religion-works, the conventional symbolic is always (at least) partially transcended and an essential spirituality is made manifest.

Religious and Aesthetic Experience

In philosophy of religion as well as in aesthetics, the notion of "experience" has, until very recently, come to dominate discussion. Among philosophers of religion, "religious experience," at least since William James's *The Varieties of Religious Experience*, has generally replaced such topics as "proofs for the existence of God"; and among philosophers of art "aesthetic experience" has been analyzed far more extensively than, say, the traditional concept of "beauty."

Now religious experience, of course, is not just of a single kind; rather it is immensely varied. Three major forms are usually distinguished: the mystical (with its several varieties), the theistic (also with its different types), and the primitive or, perhaps a better term, the "primal."[7]

To begin with the latter, and here only in the broadest and most general terms, primal religious consciousness sees regularity in experience but not lawlike or nomic structure; it sees events, as it tends to see itself, as belonging to a group and not as atomic instances or individual exemplifications of universal principles. And it sees the relations at work that constitute regularity as essentially nonmaterial and as running in various directions with all manner of dependency.

But it is not that primal religious consciousness sees things as *having* souls or spirits; it sees things as they *are* souls or spirits. Primal religious consciousness is fundamentally the mode of perception that utterly confounds the spiritual and the material—at the level of the empirical. Everything of special value that is seen is equally materially and spiritually real to it.

And so with aesthetic consciousness, in its way. Not only is the aesthetic allied to the primal in its involvement with spiritual power, the aesthetic also sees things in their startling particularity and as they are potentially numinous. Concentrating attention entirely on what is presented to it, aesthetic consciousness notices precisely that subtle web of relations that generates (in this case, a noncausal) harmony among the diverse and contrasting elements of the whole. The "aesthetic surface" of an artwork is necessarily present in its materiality.

This brings us to the kinship between the aesthetic and "theistic" religious experience—the experience of human beings in relation to and with a personal divinity who is usually taken to be a supreme, transcendent creator God. (Polytheism may here be collapsed with monotheism, for, in experiential terms, the polytheist, it is often pointed out, is in fact a henotheist; he tends to ascribe ultimacy to no more than one god at a time and to relate to that god accordingly).

At one extreme of theistic experience we have the experience of "unity," of deep communion between the self and God, a communion that is ecstatic and overwhelming. Theistic experience here borders on nonduality, but with the presence still of both subject and object, it comes within the relational order. The unity of the self and God in this the most intense loving relation is of two spirits—of which it is often said (some think blasphemously), each needs the other. Lost as the self might be in the intensity of its loving wonderment, it nevertheless is there in the full integrity of its own being.

The theistic experience, however, in its most common and basic form is one of encounter. As Rudolf Otto convincingly described it for many, the experience involves a special complex state of consciousness, one that "is perfectly *sui generis* and irreducible to any other."[8] Otto called this special state of consciousness the *numinous*; it is that which is directed to a *mysterium tremendum*. The *tremendum*, for Otto, involves such elements as "awefulness," "overpoweringness," and "urgency"; the *mysterium*, as wholly otherness with its sense of "fascination." What emerges from Otto's phenomenology of theistic experience so clearly is the presence within the experience of conflicting tensions: of attractions and repulsions, of opposing feelings such as that of great power and also utter helplessness. Nearness and estrangement become the two poles within which the experience vibrates.

Now throughout these different kinds of theistic religious experience, and obviously in varying degrees, there is that turning over of oneself to the other for the sake of completion; there is loving, faithful consciousness, a faith that is not just invoked in the experience but is part of an integral, on-going process. It is a mistake, I think, and one which is found in many analyses of experience, to assume that an experience just happens to begin at some specifiable point in X's career and that X then undergoes something he or she can subsequently reflect on as his or her "experience." This assumption leads one to neglect the fact that the most interesting and profound experiences are not episodes but processes of relationship integral to and extending throughout the development of one's personhood.

The faithful attitude that is at once formative and expressive of the person makes possible then the self-surrender or giving of self-will theistic experience requires. The self-surrender, though, is not passive in character; rather, as Otto and others like Tillich have shown, it involves an active integration of emotive, cognitive and conative dimensions: It involves the "whole person."

The experience itself then becomes an intensification of these capacities of self, and the experiencer has the sense of enhanced power. Emotionally this is expressed in the joy that is felt and also, often, in the accompanying anguish and feeling of helplessness: conatively in the feeling of liberation and freedom from the constraints otherwise operating in self-will; cognitively in the awareness of a new valuational ground for one's ideas and beliefs.

From this enhancement there follows, to whatever degree, that self-transcendence which, in its most intense form in theism, is a *conversion* of self or "new birth." The experience process culminates in a reshaping and remaking of the experiencer.

Many of these features or moments of experience are characteristic of the aesthetic as well as of the religious. To experience a work of art one must be open to it so that it may fully be for one. Unlike in theistic experience, however, a "distance" between self and object is demanded: the semblance-nature of the artwork must always be maintained in the self-giving process of the apprehension of the work's meaning.

In the experience of an artwork there is also that enhancement of the self, that exciting joy (and sometimes painful despair, alienation, spiritual dryness, and loss of confidence), liberation, and world discovery. And, most important, there is in the deepest experiences that satisfaction, that peacefulness—the *śāntarasa*, as it is called in classical Indian aesthetics—which comes from a loving participation in the work. Aesthetic experience in its most profound and moving form is a loving experience: an accepting, celebrating, affirming relation with an object whose formed content controls the response of the experiencer and for which the experiencer, in his or her own way, seeks completion.

The theist may assert God's need for oneself as well as one's need for God and one's transfiguration through the relationship; the aesthetic experiencer also finds oneself to be a new being when one is truly with that artwork whose excellence may rightly call for rejoicing.

The mention of *śāntarasa*, the "peaceful" *rasa*, the quality of serenity, harmony, fulfillment that is said, in Indian aesthetics, to be the essence of the aesthetic brings us to the "mystical."

By radically separating the concept (symbol) from the thing and by stressing the distance between the human and the divine, most of us today have lost not only the sense of divine power had by primal religious consciousness and the yearning for completion felt so intensely by the devout theist, but their profound sense of wonder as well. It is perhaps the mystical which regains and retains what is best in the primal and the theistic; and the mystical is expressed (if not wholly realized) most clearly in art.

Śāntarasa is the realization of spiritual silence that arises, at the most essential level of aesthetic experience, from the involvement with the radiant splendor, seen in wonderment, of the artwork. Religion and art here assuredly attain their highest kinship, for the aesthetic here points the way to reality and divinity. The experiencer, as well as the maker, of the artwork—at this level (which is rarely achieved but the achievement of which is the special office of art)—apprehends in and through the work his or her own being as it is in its wholeness and integrity. The apprehension of the essential in art is at once an experience of the artwork and a realization of the self. A harmony that overcomes distinction prevails, and the self knows itself as and in relation to Reality.

In sum, the artist and the saint, we have suggested to begin with, cannot do each other's work. Art and religion, although allied spiritual activities that are closely related to one another, are not the same thing.

The religion-work, whose primary function is one of leading the participant in it to distinctive religious states of being, calls precisely for a participation that goes to define the very character of the work. The religion-work involves a sense of recovery (rather than aesthetic discovery); the re-enacting of a timeless possibility (rather than the bringing of something new into being); the religion-work is a collective expression (rather than the product of an individual effort).

But art and religion may each present something of the spiritual life for response and appropriation. What makes an artwork religious, though, is not its subject matter (usually conventional cultural symbols drawn from mythico-historical experience) but its aesthetic content, as this is informed by an intuition of spiritual being. The conventional religious (or theological) cannot rightfully make any demands on art, for the sacredness of art is to be found only in its capacity to be revelatory of being. On the other side of the art/religion kinship, the aesthetic dimension of religion is found not essentially or exhaustively in an aesthetic appreciation of the formal qualities of religion-works per se, but as the religion-work is, at one end, grounded in a primal power intrinsic to the work and, at the other end, in what art itself seeks, namely, its being a form that articulates a meaning for intuition, when, that is to say, an essential spirituality is made manifest.

The experience of art and religion likewise discloses similarities and differences, with each contributing to the understanding of the other.

Primal religious experience, with its emphasis on efficacious happenings, is allied with the aesthetic insofar as the aesthetic also concentrates on nonnomic relations and sees things as they are potentially numinous.

Theistic religious experience, in its diverse forms, is also closely allied with the aesthetic in its interest in self-surrender, emotional fulfillment, and loving consciousness. Both the religious and the aesthetic are formative and expressive of a process development of the person and lead, when successful, to an enhancement of self and discovery of world. Both often vibrate with the tensions and suffering associated with the intensity of the search and subsequent realization or failure. Both kinds of experience can also point the way to an essential level of spirituality where an enduring harmony is achieved.

The "mystical" is just that level of essential spirituality where religion and art most closely meet, interrelate, and separate. The aesthetic experience, the experience of an artwork that is capable of controlling an experience and bringing it to the level of the essential, here enables the experiencer to apprehend his or her own being, through the artwork, in its wholeness and integrity. One is enabled to know oneself in relation to Reality. The religious mystic, on the other hand, is able to dispense with artworks entirely. He or she advances in that abysmal aloneness to the realization of Reality itself—until the very end.

Notes

Chapter 1. On the Question "What Is Art?"

1. Kim Levin, *Beyond Modernism: Essays on Art from the 70s and 80s* (New York: Harper & Row, 1988), p. 6.

2. Lydia Goehr, "Being True to the Work," *The Journal of Aesthetics and Art Criticism* [hereafter *JAAC*] 47, no.1 (Winter 1985): 56.

3. Frank Burch Brown, *Religious Aesthetics: A Theological Study of Making and Meaning* (Princeton, N.J.: Princeton University Press, 1989), p. 74.

4. Ibid., pp. 160–61.

5. Roland Barthes, *The Responsibility of Forms*, trans. Richard Howard (Berkeley and Los Angeles: University of California Press, 1991), p. 199.

6. For a detailed discussion of this, see Paul Oscar Kristeller's well-known article "The Modern System of the Arts," *Journal of the History of Ideas* 12, no. 4 (1951).

7. Theodor Adorno, *Aesthetic Theory*, trans. C. Lenhardt (London and New York: Routledge & Kegan Paul, 1984), p. 3.

8. One must, I think, acknowledge squarely that any theory or definition of art, including one's own, will necessarily be highly normative in character. But, if the prescriptions are tied to real possibilities of art and point to something essentially important about what we do take as works of art, then this normative character can serve a useful philosophic and critical purpose.

9. Morris Weitz, "The Role of Theory in Aesthetics," *JAAC* 15, no. 1 (September 1956): 27–35.

10. *American Philosophical Quarterly* 2, no. 3 (July 1965): 219–228.

11. Morris Weitz, "Art as an Open Concept: From *The Opening Mind*," in *Aesthetics: A Critical Anthology*, ed. George Dickie, Richard Sclafani, & Ronald Roblin, 2d ed. (New York: St. Martin's Press, 1989), p. 154.

12. Ibid., p. 159.

13. See his "The Artworld," *Journal of Philosophy* (1964): 571–84.

14. See the Preface to his *The Transfiguration of the Commonplace* (Cambridge, Mass.: Harvard University Press, 1981) and his *The Philosophical Disenfranchisement of Art* (New York: Columbia University Press, 1986).

15. George Dickie, "The New Institutional Theory of Art," in *Aesthetics: A Critical Anthology*, pp. 199–200.

16. Ibid., pp. 200 and 204.

17. Richard Wollheim, *Painting as an Art*, Bollingen Series, No. 35 (Princeton, N.J.: Princeton University Press, 1987), p. 14.

Chapter 2. Art Is Imitation

1. W. D. Ross, *Aristotle* (New York: Meridian Books, 1959), p. 269. Harvey Goldstein, in an interesting article, "Mimesis and Catharsis Reexamined" (*JAAC* 24, no. 4 [Summer 1966]: 567–77), points out, however, that even though Aristotle also used mimesis to convey the idea of copying it had for him primarily to do with an imitation of the *method* or *process* of nature and not with a representation of sense objects.

2. Plotinus, *Enneads* 5.8.1, trans. Stephen MacKenna.

3. Katherine Everett Gilbert and Helmut Kuhn, *A History of Esthetics* (Bloomington: Indiana University Press, 1953), p. 220.

4. Leo Steinberg, "The Eye Is Part of the Mind," in *Reflections on Art*, ed. Susanne K. Langer (New York: Oxford University Press, 1953), p. 220.

5. Susanne K. Langer, *Feeling and Form* (New York: Charles Scribner's Sons, 1953), p. 46.

6. E. H. Gombrich, *Art and Illusion: A Study in the Psychology of Pictorial Representation*, 2nd ed. (New York: Pantheon Books, 1960), p. 86.

7. Ibid., p. 87. In his *Meditations on a Hobby Horse* (London and New York: Phaidon Publishers, 1963), Gombrich argues that the origins of representation in art are to be found in a process of "substitution." "Substitutes," he writes, "reach deep into biological functions that are common to man and animal. The cat runs after the ball as if it were a mouse." Here, " 'representation' does not depend on formal similarities, beyond the minimum requirement of function. The ball has nothing in common with the mouse except that it is chaseable" (p. 4). And thus, "The greater the biological relevance an object has for us the more will we be attuned to its recognition—and the more tolerant will therefore be our standards of formal correspondence" (p. 7).

8. See his *The Transfiguration of the Commonplace*.

9. Steinberg, "The Eye," p. 247.

10. Ibid.

11. Mikel Dufrenne, in *The Phenomenology of Aesthetic Experience*, trans. by Edward S. Casey et al. (Evanston, Ill.: Northwestern University Press, 1973), tends, on the other hand, to insist that resemblance need not be a feature in portrayal at all, for in the experience of the artwork we come to rely completely on the aesthetic content and not the subject matter of the work. "Whether a portrait resembles its subject or not," he writes, "it is not an aesthetic object until it ceases to be a portrait and loses the signifying role which is so frequently assumed by the photograph. We should not be tempted to think in terms of a pre-existent model. The represented object must appear to result from the demands of the particular painting in which it figures. When we gaze on Franz Hal's portrait of Descartes, we should think of Hals rather than Descartes . . ." (p. 118). But surely with a portrait, the subject matter is never wholly erased by, or absorbed as such within, "the demands of the particular painting." We assume that a portrait, by its very nature, has some referential function.

We also, of course, have the situation where a portrait alters fundamentally the way in which the person portrayed is subsequently seen. Picasso is reported to have remarked on being told that his portrait of Gertrude Stein did not look like her, that she would now. The person portrayed may come to resemble the portrait!

12. Wladyslaw Tatarkiewicz, *History of Aesthetics*, ed. J. Harrel (The Hague: Mouton, 1970), vol. 1, p. 17.

13. Ibid., p. 143.

14. Ibid., p. 93.

15. This is exhibited especially in those traditions (e.g., the Confucian Chinese) where a kind of imitative continuity from one artist to another is stressed. The apprentice strives here to become like the master not through a mere repetition of the master's work but through achieving, based on that work, a distinctiveness appropriate to oneself.

16. Clive Bell, *Art* (London: Chatto & Windus, 1928), p. 16.

17. "Only through the pure contemplation . . . which ends entirely in the object, can Ideas be comprehended, and the nature of *genius* consists in pre-eminent capacity for such contemplation. Now, as this requires that a man should entirely forget himself and the relations in which he stands, *genius* is simply the completest *objectivity*, i.e., the objective tendency of the mind, as opposed to the subjective, which is directed to one's own self" (3:36).

18. See Francis Sparshott, "Imagination—The Very Idea," *JAAC* 48, no. 1 (Winter 1990): 21. See also the discussion of Aristotle in Eva T. H. Brown's comprehensive survey, *The World of the Imagination: Sum and Substance* (Savage, Md.: Rowman & Littlefield Publishers, 1991).

19. Ibid., p. 3.

20. Having an image *in* consciousness—or consciousness as imagining—is therefore not the same thing as presenting an image *for* consciousness, which is what creativity

is all about. It is precisely this objectifying activity of artistic imagination, the conjuring of a new reality as embodied insight, that distinguishes it from all imagining as such.

21. This account of imagination is, of course, exactly contra to Freud's treatment of creativity in art, insofar as Freud assumes that creativity is reducible to a kind of compensatory satisfaction seeking, a fulfillment of desires denied the artist in the real world. Art becomes then a manifestation of wish-fulfilling desires and is responded to in those terms. Cf. his "The Relation of Poet to Daydreaming." It is interesting to note that everything Freud says about art is true—for bad art or for merely popular fantasy stuff like so-called soap operas.

22. Cf. Vincent Tomas, "Creativity in Art," *The Philosophical Review* 67, no. 1 (January 1958): and Monroe C. Beardsley, "On the Creation of Art," *JAAC* 23, no. 3 (1965).

23. And hence the sense in the assertion often made that artistic creativity is an articulation or self-formation of the artist as much as it is a making of an artwork. Creativity in art forms the artist; it is a kind of self-*discovery* and self-*making*, not a mere self-*expression*. The creativity of an artist is therefore often as much a surprise to him or her as it may be a wonder to others.

Chapter 3. Art Is Expression

1. R. G. Collingwood, *The Principles of Art* (Oxford: The Clarendon Press, 1938), p. 122–23.

The expression theory of art has undergone an interesting and rather curious historical development. Spawned by romanticism's emphasis on the artist as a self-consciously creative being, with art often looked upon as a means for the artist's self-expression, the theory in its initial formulations (by Eugene Vernon, Croce, Collingwood, Ducasse) was concerned primarily with the creative process, willing as it was at times (e.g., Croce) to relegate the actual physical work of art to a secondary position. The making of an artwork, in the initial formulation, was a kind of therapy. It enabled the artist, and the experiencer of his or her art, to attain a knowledge of and, by implication, a freedom from an otherwise turbulent, inchoate emotional force.

Thinkers like Susanne K. Langer, however, recognized that, as a psychology of the creative process, the traditional expression theory is severely limited to at best a particular type of creativity and insisted, in a more sophisticated way, that the artwork may be a symbol of human feeling. The artwork then becomes an expressive form—an articulation of feeling for contemplative understanding.

It was not long before analytically oriented philosophers (Monroe Beardsley, O. K. Bouswma, John Hospers) discovered a lack of clarity in the whole notion of expression, that the terms *express, expressive,* and *expression* were used in a variety of ways. These critics shifted the whole direction of the theory away from the artist and toward the expressive values of the artwork itself by asking how we can intelligibly ascribe anthropomorphic qualities to a work of art ("sad music" as the saw or paradigm). And they concluded that the expression theory was utterly dispensable. All expression language used to talk about artworks can be translated without loss of meaning into nonexpression language (about formal qualities and subject matter).

In very recent times, however, other analytically oriented writers (Alan Tormay, *The Concept of Expression* [Princeton, N.J.: Princeton University Press, 1971]; Guy Sircello, *Mind and Art: An Essay on the Varieties of Expression* [Princeton, N.J.: Princeton University Press, 1972]) have tried to rescue the theory by appealing to various ways in which anthropomorphic predicates can be applied to works of art in a manner unlike their application to natural objects and thus to show how *expression, expressive of,* and *expressing* are necessary for aesthetic analysis. The emphasis, however, still remains on how it can be said that a work of art is expressive of certain human emotions. The theory is perhaps ready now for a more basic reconstruction—at the roots.

2. John Hospers. "The Concept of Artistic Expression," reprinted with some changes by the author in *Problems of Aesthetics*, ed. Morris Weitz (New York: Macmillan Co., 1970).

3. Ibid., p. 227.

4. Alasdair MacIntyre, *Whose Justice? Which Rationality?* (Notre Dame, Ind.: University of Notre Dame Press, 1988), p. 76.

5. See my *Creative Being: The Crafting of Person and World* (Honolulu: University of Hawaii Press, 1992), Chapter 3.

6. M. Hiriyanna, *Art Experience* (Mysore: Kavyalaya Publishers, 1954), p. 34.

7. *Abhinavabhāratī*, in Raniero Gnoli, *The Aesthetic Experience According to Abhinavagupta*, 2d ed. (Varanasi: Chowkhama Sanskrit Series Office, 1968), p. 81.

8. V. K. Chari, *Sanskrit Criticism* (Honolulu: University of Hawaii Press, 1990), p. 62.

9. Zeami and his father, Kwannami Kiyotsuyu (1333–1384), are usually credited with the "invention" of Nō, the most sophisticated and subtle form of theater in Japan. and perhaps in the world. For good introductions to Nō and Zeami's contributions, see Donald Keene, ed., *20 Plays of the Nō Theater* (New York and London: Columbia University Press, 1970); Arthur Waley, *The Nō Plays of Japan* (New York: Grove Press, 1957); and Japanese Translations Committee, Nippon Gakujutsu Shinōkai, *The Noh Drama* (Tokyo and Rutland: Charles E. Tuttle Company, 1955).

10. Zeami's "treatises" on Nō were discovered only in 1908. See *Sources of Japanese Tradition*, compiled by Ryusaku Tsunoda, Wm. Theodore de Bary, and Donald Keene (New York: Columbia University Press, 1958), pp. 288–91.

11. René Sieffert, *La tradition secrète du No* (Paris: Gallimard, 1960), p. 53.

12. Japanese Translation Committee, *The Noh Drama*, pp. ix–x.

13. Makoto Ueda, *Literary and Art Theories in Japan* (Cleveland: The Press of Western Reserve University, 1967), p. 60.

14. Peter Lamarque, "Expression and the Mask: The Dissolution of Personality in Noh," *JAAC* 47, no. 2 (Spring 1989): 157.

15. Ibid., p. 159.

16. Ibid., p. 161.

17. Ibid., p. 166.

18. Ibid., p. 163.

19. Ibid.

20. For a further discussion of the *rasa* theory and Zeami's understanding of *yūgen*, see my *Essays in Comparative Aesthetics* (Honolulu: University of Hawaii Press, 1975).

21. It should be noted, of course, that with a drama, a film, a novel we do tend to respond aesthetically to specific emotional situations (say, a character showing anger within a particular action or scene) in much the same way as we do with actual life situations, noting the appropriateness of the emotion and so on; but even here we also recognize that the emotionality so presented is only internal to the dynamics of the work itself. It exists nowhere else but in the work.

22. H. H. Arnason, *History of Western Art*, 3d ed., revised and updated by Daniel Wheeler (Englewood Cliffs, N.J.: Prentice-Hall, and New York: Harry N. Abrams, 1986), p. 83.

23. Susanne K. Langer, from *Problems in Art* in *A Modern Book of Esthetics*, ed. Melvin Rader, 4th ed. (New York: Holt, Rinehart & Winston, 1973), p. 296.

24. Leonard B. Meyer, *Emotion and Meaning in Music* (Chicago: University of Chicago Press, 1956), p. 34.

25. Octavio Paz, *The Bow and the Lyre*, trans. Ruth L. C. Simms (Austin: University of Texas Press, 1973), p. 142.

26. Langer, *Feeling and Form*, p. 311.

27. Anthony Savile, "Beauty: A Neo-Kantian Account," in *Essays in Kant's Aesthetics*, ed. Ted Cohen & Paul Guyer (Chicago and London: The University of Chicago Press, 1982), p. 116.

28. Ibid.

29. Kant is basically concerned with what he calls *free beauty* as contrasted with "dependent" or "adherent beauty," with the former to be found essentially only in nature and in decorative artifacts. Determined as he was to liberate aesthetic judgment from all concepts, Kant was therefore unable to take adequately into account the important cognitive/interpretative dimensions of art and our experience of its more profound "beauty," which does indeed include those dimensions. Beauty in art, Kant was unable to see, is not an isolable formal play of elements; it is rather the full aesthetic content as realized in consummate form.

30. Guy Sircello, "Beauty in Shards and Fragments," *JAAC* 48, no. 1 (Winter 1990).

31. When we talk about a culture's "standard of beauty," we are usually talking about the way in which certain subject matters are to be treated—e.g., the depiction of a woman's body (as in India, narrow-waisted, large-breasted . . .) or purely formal considerations, e.g., preferences for symmetry or asymmetry, bold or subdued patterns, filled or empty spaces, and so on. In any given culture, these become the conditions for the apprehension of beauty qua beauty in art and not merely its constituents; which is to say, for any given culture a certain set of expectations regarding subject matter treatment and formal elements might have to be satisfied before the artwork as such is perceived by many in that culture to be right for itself.

Chapter 4. Aesthetic Experience and the Artwork

1. Nelson Goodman, in his *Languages of Art* (New York: The Bobbs-Merrill Co., 1968), raises the interesting question about the "localization" of a work of art. He argues that "a musical score is a notation and defines a work; that a sketch or picture is not in a notation but is itself a work; and that a literary script is both a notation and is itself a work. Thus in the different arts a work is differently localized. In painting, the work is an individual object; and in etching, a class of objects. In music, the work is the class of performances compliant with a character. In literature, the work is the character itself. And in calligraphy, we may add, the work is an individual inscription" (p. 210).

What Goodman fails to realize is that an artwork, as localized, is always in a particular cultural context and that this context is part of the identification of the work qua particular, localized work, indicating as it does in what way it is appropriate to respond to the work. If we had a case of two apparently identical works (in terms of their sensuous presentation) from different cultures, it would nevertheless make perfectly good sense to say that they might not be the *same* work. See Anthony Savile, "Nelson Goodman's 'Languages of Art: A Study,' " *The British Journal of Aesthetics* (11, no. 1 (Winter 1971), for an interesting analysis of this point.

2. It might appear that there is a confusion here insofar as, on the one hand, I have stated that what defines art is its own intentionality to be aesthetically forceful, meaningful, and beautiful and, on the other hand, that a right conception of art requires that we see the creative process, the artwork, and its apprehension as an experiential unity. The confusion, I think, is only apparent, for just as one can adopt for various purposes a telological mode of classification for natural kinds (the *telos* or structure of normality of a fish being different from that of a rock) and, without contradiction, at the same time argue that the actual human experience of any particular object (a tree, one's neighbor, an airplane) involves certain perceptual and conceptual categories, so one can argue for there being a special intentionality of what we call art and, at the same time, insist that for a right undertanding of art this intentionality must be brought into the matrix of any particular work's process of coming into being and of the conditions and manner in which it is properly experienced aesthetically.

3. In a famous essay " 'Psychical Distance' as a Factor in Art and an Aesthetic Principle" (*British Journal of Psychology* 5 [1912]), Edward Bullough argued that aesthetic

experience demands the imposition of a certain distance "between our own self and its affections" or "between our self and such objects as are the sources or vehicles of such affections." This distance is obtained, Bullough says, "by separating the object and its appeal from one's own self, by putting it out of gear with practical needs and ends." He goes on to say that "Distance does not imply an impersonal, purely intellectually interested relation of such a kind. On the contrary, it describes a *personal* relation, often highly emotionally colored, but of a *peculiar character.* Its peculiarity lies in that the personal character of the relation has been, so to speak, filtered. It has been cleared of the practical, concrete nature of its appeal, without, however, thereby losing its original constitution." He concludes by postulating an "antinomy of Distance"; namely, that "What is therefore, both for appreciation and production, most desirable is *the utmost decrease of Distance without its disappearance.*" This allows the participant to be deeply involved with the artwork yet able to relate with it precisely as it is a work of art. Now, although there are many ambiguities and difficulties in this notion of a "psychical distance," it—or something like it—has become widely accepted as describing the *attitude* appropriate to our experience of aesthetic objects.

4. Clive Bell, *Art*, p. 4.

Chapter 6. Temporality and the Visual Arts

1. By *normal range*, and of course we do not want to make too much of this, we mean only that any particular work has, in terms of its complexity, subtlety, and the rest, a time in which it may most naturally be experienced rightly. Some works, say Giorgione's *Tempest* or a typical Southern Sung painting, which invites the spectator to move about in the landscape, call for a more extended time for their apprehension than do others, say a typical Mondrian abstract painting.

2. Paul Klee, *On Modern Art*, trans. Paul Findlay (London: Faber & Faber, 1948), p. 16.

3. Ibid., p. 17.

4. Mikel Dufrenne, *The Phenomenology of Aesthetic Experience*, trans. Edward S. Casey et al. (Evanston, Ill.: Northwestern University Press, 1973), p. 292.

Chapter 7. Mallarmé and Valéry and the Essence of Poetry

1. Although there are many differences between Mallarmé and Valéry in their personalities as well as their work, we group them together here without distinction because of their common stance toward creativity and poetry. Valéry explicitly acknowledges his debt to Mallarmé, and especially in his early verse, Valéry closely follows the program for purity outlined by Mallarmé.

2. Paul Valéry, *The Art of Poetry*, trans. by Denise Folliot, Bollingen Series No. 45 (New York: Pantheon Books, 1958), p. 183.

3. *Mallarmé: Selected Prose Poems, Essays and Letters*, trans. Bradford Cook (Baltimore: The John Hopkins Press, 1956), p. 43.

4. Ibid., p. 40.

5. Valéry, *The Art of Poetry*, p. 102.

6. Wallace Fowlie, *Mallarmé* (Chicago: The University of Chicago Press, 1953), p. 233.

7. Ibid., p. 19.

8. Paul Valéry, *Selected Writings* (this section translated by Louise Verèse), (New York: New Directions, 1950), p. 143.

9. Valéry, *The Art of Poetry*, p. 116.

10. "Gift of a Poem," in Stéphane Mallarmé, *Poems*, trans. Roger Fry (New York: New Directions, 1951), p. 59.

11. Valéry, *The Art of Poetry*, p. 55.

12. Isabel Hungerland, "Language and Poetry," *The University of California Publications in Philosophy* 33 (1958).

13. A perfect example of this is Mallarmé's *Un Coup De Dés*, where the physical placement of words on the page is to be a central factor in the experience of the poem's form. But the real form of a poem is always apprehended inwardly, it is not seen by the eye as such.

It might be of interest here to contrast briefly Mallarmé's and Valéry's program for poetry with that traditional form of Japanese poetry that, on the surface at least, most closely resembles it; namely, the haiku. Harold G. Henderson has noted that "in the hands of a master a haiku can be the concentrated essence of pure poetry." *An Introduction to Haiku: An Anthology of Poems and Poets from Bashō to Shiki* (New York: Doubleday Anchor Books, 1958), p. 2. Henderson also points out that the haiku "usually gain their effect not only by suggesting a mood, but also by giving a clear-cut picture which serves as a starting point for trains of thought and emotion" (ibid., p. 3). Whereas Mallarmé and Valéry would have poetic suggestiveness constitute, as far as possible, the poem itself, the master of the haiku rightly recognizes that the poem must be wed to experience. Mallarmé and Valéry wanted to subtract ordinary cognitive associations from language to express the essence of poetry. Haiku simply employs an economy of expression, within a strict form, to enter directly into the essence of experience and to achieve maximum suggestiveness.

Chapter 8. Where Is a Dance?

1. Susanne K. Langer, *Feeling and Form*, p. 190.

2. John J. Martin, *An Introduction to the Dance* (New York: W. W. Norton & Company, 1939), p. 66.

3. The "instruments" for movement in dance, of course, vary considerably from culture to culture; in Asian dance traditions especially, there is extensive use of eye

movements, symbolic arm and leg gestures (the *mudrās*), and so on as well as the use of the feet.

4. See *JAAC* 39, no. 4 (Summer 1981): 399–408.

Chapter 9. Form in Architecture

1. In architecture, perhaps more than in any other art, we have what we might call "impress" art—works whose primary function is to impress the viewer with the wealth, power, status and the like of the "possessor" of the work (whether an individual, an institution, a state) and that have been created with this intention and do embody it. Almost all works of monumental size tend to come under this category, whether they be celebratory (gigantic Buddha statues) or inhibitory (Stalinist state buildings). And although the realization of form in architecture, as I will try to show, is independent in many crucial ways from social or political factors, with "impress" art we have such a predominance of dictates regarding shape that it becomes extremely difficult for rightness in the relationship between shape and structure to obtain.

2. The term *postmodernism*, as is often recognized, has come to mean many different things to many different people—some see it as a wholesale rejection of the modern (especially those of a deconstructivist bent with their tirades against "logocentrism"), others, as the last phase of the modern and thus in some kind of continuity with it. There is, however, some considerable agreement that for architecture "postmodernism" received its earliest and clearest pronouncement in the writings of Robert Venturi (most notably his *Complexity and Contradiction in Architecture*, 1966 and *Learning from Las Vegas: The Forgotten Symbolism of Architectural Forms*, which he edited with Denise Scott Brown and Steven Izemour in 1988), where he categorically rejects the modernist program for architecture.

3. Venturi writes: "When it cast out eclecticism, Modern architecture submerged symbolism. Instead it promoted expressionism, concentrating on the expression of architectural elements themselves: on the expression of structure and function. . . . By limiting itself to strident articulation of the pure architectural elements of space, structure, and program, Modern architecture's expression has become a dry expressionism, empty and boring—and in the end irresponsible." *Learning from Las Vegas* (Cambridge, Mass., and London: The MIT Press, 1972, 1977), pp. 101–3.

4. Or an environment might grow around and about a building so as to confound and distort any possible aesthetically meaningful relationship between them (as with the Duomo in Florence, Italy).

5. Architects often speak of the factors that "drive a design" and pay special attention to, or concern for, the programmatic requirements which the building must fulfill—its functioning as a house, a bank, an office complex, and so on, and "within budget"—and how the building will both adjust to and alter a given environment. Various cultural traditions have, of course, also placed greater or less emphasis on the relationship between a building and its natural, organic place—e.g., the intimate relationship between

house and garden that is stressed in much of traditional Japanese architecture, and which relationship becomes integral to the determination of shape and the recognition of form—nevertheless, it is clearly the case that all buildings bear a "transactional" relationship with their sites that becomes a special element in the building's shape.

Chapter 10. Music as Silence-and-Sound

1. Leonard B. Meyer, "On Rehearing Music," *Journal of the American Musicological Society* 14, no. 2 (1961): 260.

2. *Politics*, 1340a.

Chapter 11. Interpreting Art

1. Arthur C. Danto, *The Transfiguration of the Commonplace*, p. 98.

2. Rainer Maria Rilke, *Duino Elegies*, trans. J. B. Leishman and Stephen Spender (New York: W. W. Norton & Company, 1939), "First Elegy," lines 1–2.

3. *Duino Elegies*, Commentary, p. 89.

4. This does not mean that interpretation need involve the looking for a subtext, hidden by the literal or phenomenal text, that is assumed to contain the real meaning of the work; rather it may rightly involve only the quite natural seeing of connections within the text that constitute its aesthetic content and the way in which these connections lead as well to life meanings, to our experience as persons in the world.

5. Umberto Eco, *The Limits of Interpretation* (Bloomington and Indianapolis: Indiana University Press, 1990), p. 21.

6. As Schleiermacher noted in his "Outline of the 1819 Lectures" (*Die Kompendienartige Darstellung von 1819*), "No individual inspection of a work exhausts its meaning; interpretation can always be rectified." (II, 4).

7. See his *Truth and Method*, revised trans. Joel Weinsheimer and Donald G. Marshall (New York: Crossroad, 1989).

8. *Duino Elegies*, "First Elegy," lines 68–84.

9. Ibid., Commentary, p. 93.

10. Dilthey went so far as to assert that "The ultimate goal of the hermeneutic process is to understand an author better than he understood himself." (See his *Die Entstehung der Hermeneutik.*) We would say that "the hermeneutic process" is to understand the *work* in ways different from what may have been intended by its author and that the New Critics' belief "in the relative autonomy of verbal [or pictorial] configurations from conscious intentions in a thinker, speaker, or writer" so that "combinations of words seem sometimes *of themselves* to urge upon us new meanings" (Richard Strier, "The Poetics of Surrender: An Exposition and Critique of New Critical

Poetics," *Critical Inquiry* 2, no. 1 [Autumn 1975]: 172) is correct so long as the "relative" in "the relative autonomy of verbal configurations . . ." is properly understood and emphasized.

11. Jacques Derrida, *Speech and Phenomena*, trans. David B. Allison (Evanston, Ill.: Northwestern University Press, 1973), p. 139.

12. Ibid.

13. Christofer Norris and Andrew Benjamin, *What Is Desconstruction?* (London and New York: St. Martin's Press, Academy Editions, 1988), p. 12.

14. Ibid., p. 18.

15. Nelson Goodman, "How Buildings Mean", in *Aesthetics: A Critical Anthology*, ed. George Dickie, Richard Scalfani, Ronald Roblin, 2d ed. (New York: St. Martin's Press, 1989), p. 553.

16. Ibid., p. 554.

17. Hans-Georg Gadamer, *The Relevance of the Beautiful: And Other Essays*, ed. Robert Bernasconi, trans. Nicholas Walker (Cambridge: Cambridge University Press, 1986), p. 33.

18. Paul Ricoeur rightly notes that "dream symbolism can in no way be a simple play of meanings, referring back and forth among themselves; it is the milieu of expression where desire is uttered" (*The Conflict of Interpretations*, trans. Kathleen McLaughlin [Evanston, Ill.: Northwestern University Press, 1974], p. 66).

19. *Duino Elegies*, "Second Elegy," lines 1–3.

20. Ibid., Commentary, p. 94.

21. See *Against Interpretation: And Other Essays* (New York: Noonday Press, 1966).

22. Danto, *The Transfiguration of the Commonplace*, p. 113.

Chapter 12. Truth in Art

1. This is the conventional (and oversimplified) account of Plato's position, which needs, of course, to be tempered somewhat by taking into account his wider concerns about the relationships between the artist, the poet in particular, and the philosopher, and his extolling the idea and experience of beauty as set forth in the *Symposium*. For a helpful account, see Whitney L. Oates, *Plato's View of Art* (New York: Charles Scribner's Sons, 1972), chap. 1; and Iris Murdoch, *The Fire and the Sun: Why Plato Banished the Artists* (Oxford: Oxford University Press, 1977).

2. *Poetics*, 1460. trans. Ingram Bywater.

3. Bertram E. Jessup ("Truth as Material in Art," *JAAC* 4, no. 2 [Winter 1945]); F. E. Sparshott ("Truth in Fiction," *JAAC* 26, no. 1 [Fall 1967]); and James K. Feibleman

("The Truth Value of Art." *JAAC* 24, no. 4 [Summer 1966]), for example, support, in varying ways, the position that truth in art is aesthetically relevant, with Sparshott arguing the larger case that imagination, via memory, always works with the actual world so that "truth" is always relevant in art, and Feibleman that there are many truth values in art (the truth value of coherence, when the work has unity, as well as correspondence, when it deals with the "axiological aspects of facts").

Somewhat greater weight, though, seems to be cast on the other side of the argument. Douglas N. Morgan ("Must Art Tell the Truth," *JAAC* 26, no. 1 [Fall 1967]) among many others, has forcefully argued that "truth" indeed pertains only to propositions, but that art does not need justification on truth grounds at all: Its value as beauty is sufficient. Albert William Levi ("Literary Truth," *JAAC* 24, no. 3 [Spring 1966]), following somewhat more closely the position I. A. Richards put forth in *Science and Poetry* (1926) and *Principles of Literary Criticism* (1925), takes the same line and insists that "truth" rightly belongs to logic and science and that it is a category mistake to apply it to art (literature). "Meaning" and "significance" are different from "truth" and do apply to the autonomous domain of the creative imagination.

Kingsley Price ("Is There Aesthetic Truth," *Journal of Philosophy* 66, no. 2 [May 1949]) ("works of art do not mean other things to which they might be true"); Sidney Zink ("Poetry and Truth," *Philosophical Review* 54, no. 2 [1945]) ("Truth is not something to be contemplated, nor even something to be "enforced," in the sense of persuaded. Truth is rather to be discovered or verified. And because it is not the business of poetry to discover or verify, poems *as* poems, are neither true nor false"); and Louis Arnaud Reid ("Art, Truth and Reality," *British Journal of Aesthetics* 4, no. 4 [October 1964]) ("Whereas the criterion of truth as likeness sets up a prior model of natural fact to which the picture is supposed to correspond, just the reverse happens when the art is good. The art itself becomes and sets the standard by which the world is seen in a new way"), together with more recent hermeneutical analysis (Gadamer), develop this position further.

4. Eliot Deutsch, *On Truth: An Ontological Theory* (Honolulu: University of Hawaii Press, 1979), p. 2.

5. Some might argue that Hegel articulated the more radical notion of truth, albeit he did not integrate it as such into his thinking about "truth in art." Hegel distinguished rather sharply between "correctness"—or that "correspondence" which most philosophers take to be the sense of truth—and "truth" proper. "In common life," he writes, "the terms *truth* and *correctness* are often treated as synonymous: we speak of the truth of a content, when we are only thinking of its correctness. Correctness, generally speaking, concerns only the formal coincidence between our conception and its content, whatever the constitution of this content may be. Truth, on the contrary, lies in the coincidence of the object with itself, that is, with its notion [*Begriff*]. That a person is sick, or that someone has committed a theft, may certainly be correct. But the content is untrue. A sick body is not in harmony with the notion of body" (*The Logic of Hegel*, trans. William Wallace, from the *Encyclopaedia of the Philosophical Sciences* [Oxford: The Clarendon Press, 1892], p. 305).

The "notion" of a thing, for Hegel, is the essential, defining quality of that thing, what the thing is supposed to be in our conception of it. As in the ancient Confucian doctrine of the "rectification of names," things are properly themselves only when they are what they should be according to their nature as they are conceived. And therefore, in his *Phenomenology of Mind*, Hegel is able to say that "truth finds the medium of its existence in notions and conceptions alone." Now, for Hegel, of course, this conception of truth has its meaning only in the larger metaphysical schema, where truth is determined relative to the advancement of the Absolute or the *Idea* as the rational structure of reality. Nevertheless, apart from the questionable rationalistic monism that underlies it, Hegel's conception makes for an unresolved cleavage between "correctness" and ontological coherence; and, perhaps more important, it presupposes that things have notions somehow separable from, that is, may be determined conceptually (albeit they may not be realized existentially) externally to, their concrete particularity. A "sick body" may indeed, under appropriate conditions and circumstances, be seen as what is right for a person and a contributing factor to the truth of that person's being.

6. J. L. Mehta, *Martin Heidegger: The Way and the Vision* (Honolulu: The University of Hawaii Press, 1976), p. 189.

7. Martin Heidegger, "On the Essence of Truth," trans. R. F. C. Hull and Alan Crick, in *Existence and Being*, ed. Werner Brock (Chicago: Henry Regnery Co., 1949), p. 322.

8. Ibid., pp. 328–29.

9. Ibid., p. 329.

10. Albert Hofstadter, *Truth and Art* (New York: Columbia University Press, 1965), p. 92.

11. Martin Heidegger, "The Origin of the Work of Art," in *Poetry, Language, Thought*, trans. Albert Hofstadter (New York: Harper & Row Publishers, 1971), pp. 33–34.

12. Ibid., p. 36.

13. Mehta, *Heidegger*, p. 190.

14. Dorothy Walsh, "The Cognitive Content of Art," *The Philosophical Review* 52, no. 4 (September 1943).

15. Albert Hofstadter, *Truth in Art*, pp. 195–96.

16. Ibid., p. 140

17. Roderick Chisholm developed a "linguistic version" of Brentano's thesis in his effort to set forth criteria for the intentional use of language; that is, language that refers to certain psychological states. "Intentionality" here has fundamentally to do with our way of talking about various kinds of mental phenomena. Cf. "Sentences About

Believing," in *Minnesota Studies in the Philosophy of Science*, ed. H. Feigl, M. Scriven, and G. Maxwell (Minneapolis: University of Minnesota Press, 1958), vol. 2.

18. Susanna Winkworth, trans., *Theologia Germanica* (New York: Pantheon Books, 1949), p. 124.

19. We must, of course, allow for the situation where one might be so repulsed by a worldview or particular subject matter represented (say a graphic depiction of a horrible act of infanticide) that one simply rejects the work from the start. In this case, though, it is not a matter of disagreeing with the work aesthetically because of its view; it is a matter of not getting to the work as an aesthetic object in the first place.

20. *Time* (24 January 1955), p. 72.

21. Alan White, *Truth* (New York: Doubleday & Co., Anchor Books, 1970), p. 115.

22. We may for our purpose leave aside distinctions that may be made between "forgeries," "fakes," "exact copies," and so on, for the general argument about authenticity should cut across all those distinctions.

23. In his careful analysis of the problem of forgeries, Nelson Goodman shows very nicely how knowledge of the fact of a forgery, where there is no perceptual difference between the original and the forgery, nevertheless can make for an aesthetic difference, because the knowledge "(1) stands as evidence that there may be a difference between them that I can learn to perceive, (2) assigns the present looking a role as training toward such a perceptual discrimination, and (3) makes consequent demands that modify and differentiate my present experience in looking at the two pictures" (*Languages of Art*, p. 105). Goodman, however, draws the curious conclusion that the "aesthetic difference" does not mean that an original is necessarily better than the forgery ("a copy of a Lastman by Rembrandt may well be better than the original"); and this confusion, I believe, arises once again from Goodman's failure to relize that an artwork is definable only when taking into account the creative process that brought it into being and the experience appropriate to it. The artwork, we have argued, is a process and a completion; it is grounded, it is rooted, in its "existential conditions." A forgery can never properly fulfill the intentionality of art. A master artist does not "copy" another work (if he did so as some sort of exercise, he would not regard it as a work); he may seek to be influenced by another work or artist, but the "own work," which may then be superior to an "original," is precisely a new work and not a copy of something else. It would have its own authenticity.

24. A similar situation exists in those cases where one is fooled by an artwork in taking it for the "real" thing. The critic Harold Rosenberg states the situation nicely in this way: "The interval during which a painting is mistaken for the real thing, or a real thing for a painting, is the triumphant moment of trompe l'oeil art. The artist appears to be as potent as nature, if not superior to it. Almost immediately, though, the spectator's uncertainty is eliminated by his recognition that the counterfeit is counterfeit. Once the illusion is dissolved, what is left is an object that is interesting, not as a work of art, but as a successful simulation of something that is not art. The

major response to it is curiosity" ("The Art World: Reality Again," *The New Yorker* [5 February 1972], p. 88).

25. White, *Truth*, p. 118.

Chapter 13. Art and Morality

1. Sidney Zink, "The Moral Effect of Art," *Ethics* 40 (1950): 261–74.

2. William H. Gass, "Goodness Knows Nothing of Beauty: On the Distance between Morality and Art," in *Reflecting on Art*, ed. John Andrew Fisher (Mountain View, Calif.: Mayfield Publishing Company, 1993), p. 115.

3. N. I. Bukharin, "Art and Social Evolution," in *Marxism and Art*, ed. Berel Lang and Forrest Williams (New York: David McKay Company, 1972), p. 101.

4. "Politics and the purity of art" clearly takes on different faces with respect to the particular arts. Music, on the whole, is certainly more immune to delivering political messages (albeit a Prokofiev and others could once be banned from the USSR) than say film, where all manner of controversial subject matter can vividly be set forth. Literature, drama, and other "narrative" arts lean toward film; architecture and other kinds of craft, lean toward music in the degree of their susceptibility to depict politically charged themes.

It should also be noted, of course, that modern forms of totalitarianism such as indeed are to be found in the former Soviet Union and (Marxist) China demanded the right to enlist artists in the class struggle and to use art to foster social-political solidarity. Mao Tse-Tung could happily write (in this context the "enemy" being the Japanese imperialism of the time) that our purpose is "precisely to ensure that literture and art fit well into the whole revolutionary machine as a component part, that they operate as powerful weapons for uniting and educating the people and for attacking and destroying the enemy, and that they help the people fight the enemy with one heart and mind" ("On Literature and Art," in *Marxism and Art*, p. 109).

5. Milan Kundera, *The Art of the Novel*, trans. from the French Linda Asher (New York: Harper & Row Publishers, 1988), p. 158.

6. Ibid., p. 161.

7. We also have the interesting situation where a morally repugnant viewpoint can be so transformed into aesthetic content that it no longer *appears* to be what it is. Referring to "Leni Riefenstahl's *The Triumph of the Will* and *The Olympiad* masterpieces," Susan Sontag states that, "through Riefenstahl's genius as a film-maker, the [Nazi] 'content' has—let us even assume, against her intentions[?]—come to play a purely formal role" (*Against Interpretation*, p. 26). The "moral" question then becomes one that is directed simply to the artist: Ought one to so *apparently* erase an objectionable content in one's art? I emphasize *appears* and *apparently* for one must assume that something of that viewpoint as such does remain, and purposively so, in the work and allows for

an "accepting" attitude by the viewer. If this were not so, then, of course, there would be no problem in the first place.

8. See *Critique of Judgment*, 59.

9. Susan Sontag does, however, argue a Kantian-like position with respect to our experience of art when stating that "our response to art is 'moral' insofar as it is, precisely, the enlivening of our sensibility and consciousness. Art," she goes on to say, "performs this 'moral' task because the qualities which are intrinsic to the aesthetic experience (disinterestedness, contemplativeness, attentiveness, the awakening of the feelings) and to the aesthetic object (grace, intelligence, expressiveness, energy, sensuousness) are also fundamental constituents of the moral response to life" (*Against Interpretation*, p. 25).

Another way of putting this might be to say that, where art and life come together in the fullest and best way, we are able to bring the qualities of style rooted in art (its freedom, rightness, grace, harmony) into our life actions, values, and attitudes. This is not an "aestheticizing" of life, a reduction of everything to formal qualities, an annihilation of content, but rather an elevating of consciousness in relation to world in such a way that an enhanced sensitivity is brought to bear on everything in our world; we would have, in short, the achievement of creative play as that which informs all action. But this takes us some distance from the problem of the relationship between art and morality as such.

10. Benedetto Croce, "Aesthetics," *Encyclopaedia Britannica*, 14th edition (Chicago, 1938), Vol. I, p. 265.

11. Kuo Hsi, *An Essay on Landscape Painting*, trans. Shio Sakanishi (London: John Murray, 1935), p. 48.

12. Ibid., pp. 49–50.

13. The monumental egotism of certain artists (Picasso, in most recent times) and their sometimes crude violation of established modes of ethical behavior (from betrayal of friends to outright exploitation of others) is all too prevalent to accept as universal the Chinese understanding of the necessary relationship between "virtue" and artistic performance. It may very well be the case, however, that this "egotism" has its roots in the modern Western view of creativity as having to bring something radically new into being. It is as if the artist were called upon to recognize most vividly that there is a lack in history, a void that needs to be filled, all of which implies that the whole of human culture requires his or her creative activity to redress itself. It is hardly surprising then that from this idea of creativity the artist might acquire an extraordinary sense of self-importance. It might also very well be that we need to retrieve a good deal from the traditional Chinese view of the person made evident in his or her work as a means of overcoming the silly obsession with "novelty" that has come to be confounded with "originality" and has dominated so much of the creation and "appreciation" of contemporary Western art.

14. We need, not, however, I think, go so far as Theodor Adorno does when writing that "Politically progressive critics have accused *l'art pour l'art*, many exponents of

which were in fact in league with reactionary political interests, of fetishizing the concept of the pure, self-sufficient work of art. This indictment is valid in that works of art are products of social labour. . . . In purely formal terms, prior to any analysis of what they express, art works are ideological because they *a priori* posit a spiritual entity as though it were independent of any conditions of material production, hence as though it were intrinsically superior to those conditions" (*Aesthetic Theory*, trans. C. Lenhardt [London and New York: Routledge & Kegan Paul, 1984], p. 323). If all works of art (and, it would seem, any product of human labor) thus inevitably have this "ideological" character, then one is at a loss to even begin to evaluate, as Adorno clearly wants to, the moral quality of individual works of art. Would it follow from what he has said that the more purely abstract a work of art the more it is morally suspect?

15. John Dewey, *Art as Experience* (New York: Minton, Bulch & Company, 1934), p. 105.

16. Rita Zelski, *Beyond Feminist Aesthetics: Feminist Literature and Social Change* (Cambridge, Mass.: Harvard University Press, 1989), p. 30.

17. Gadamer, *The Relevance of the Beautiful*, p. 39.

18. Gyorgy Lukács, "Art as Self-Consciousness in Man's Development," in *Marxism and Art*, p. 233.

Chapter 14. Religion and Art

1. Kenneth Clark, *Landscape Into Art* (Boston: Beacon Press, 1967), pp. 24–25.

2. Hence the difficulty that some recent feminist religionists have had in creating new forms of ritual practice appropriate to what they take to be goddess worship. Rituals that endure seem historically to evolve and not arise full-blown ex nihilo.

3. Albert Hofstadter, *Agony and Epitah* (New York: George Braziller, 1977), p. 66.

4. Jacques Maritain, *Art and Scholasticism: With Other Essays*, trans. J. F. Scanlan (New York: Charles Scribner's Sons, 1954), p. 111.

5. Hofstadter, *Agony and Epitaph*, p. 58.

6. See my *On Truth: An Ontological Theory* (Honolulu: The University Press of Hawaii, 1979), chap. 1.

7. Many historians of religions and anthropologists, to avoid the pejorative senses of *primitive* as "savage," "childish," "ill-developed," and so on proffer the more neutral definition of *primitive religion* as just the religion of people in "primitive societies." John B. Noss, for example, defines *primitive religion* in terms of "those smaller, less informed, and more isolated societies whose technology is not as highly developed as in 'civilized' societies and whose religious systems are regarded by all in the group, without exception, as indispensable to social harmony and satisfactory adaptation to the immediate environment" (*Man's Religions*, 3d ed. [New York: The Macmillan

Company, 1963], p. 3). Edwin A. Burtt also defines primitive religion in much the same way. See his *Man Seeks the Divine* (New York: Harper & Brothers, 1957), p. 35. For purposes of philosophical understanding, however, primitive religion or religious consciousness can perhaps best be taken as an ideal type or model of a certain kind of experience; namely, one that is closest to the origins of religion and yet may be present, either wholly or partially, at any historical period or "stage." Wilhelm Dupré, in *Religion in Primitive Cultures: A Study in Ethnophilosophy* (The Hague: Mounton, 1975), for example, offers a comprehensive analysis from an anthropological-hermeneutic perspective on the role of religion in primitive cultures. "Primitive religion," he tries to show, "has to be understood as the truth of religion with respect to its initial integration into the cultural process" (p. 36). More recently, John Hick in *An Interpretation of Religion: Human Responses to the Transcendent* (New Haven, Conn.: Yale University Press, 1989) distinguishes rather sharply between a "pre-axial" and a "post-axial" religiosity, including in the former all kinds of "archaic" forms. "Pre-axial" religion, Hick writes, is "centrally (but not solely) concerned with the preservation of cosmic and social order, and post-axial religion centrally (but not solely) concerned with the quest for salvation or liberation" (p. 22).

8. Rudolf Otto, *The Idea of the Holy*, trans. John W. Harvey (New York: Oxford University Press, 1958), p. 7.

Index